RISK, VULNERABILITY AND EVERYDAY LIFE

It is now sociological common sense to declare that, in everyday life, large numbers of people approach matters of work, family life, trust and friendship with 'risk' constantly in mind. This book provides an introductory overview and critical assessment of this phenomenon. Iain Wilkinson outlines contrasting sociological theories of risk, and summarises some of the principle discoveries of empirical research conducted into the ways people perceive, experience and respond to a world of danger. He also examines some of the moral concerns and political interests that feature in this area of study.

Designed to equip readers not only with the sociological means to debate the human consequences of our contemporary culture of risk, but also with the critical resources to evaluate the significance this holds for current sociology, this book provides a perfectly pitched undergraduate introduction to the topic.

Iain Wilkinson is Senior Lecturer at the School of Social Policy, Sociology and Social Research at the University of Kent. His publications include *Anxiety in a Risk Society* (2001) and *Suffering: A Sociological Introduction* (2005).

THE NEW SOCIOLOGY

SERIES EDITOR: ANTHONY ELLIOTT, FLINDERS UNIVERSITY, AUSTRALIA

The New Sociology is a book series designed to introduce students to new issues and themes in social sciences today. What makes the series distinctive, as compared with other competing introductory textbooks, is a strong emphasis not just on key concepts and ideas but on how these play out in everyday life – on how theories and concepts are lived at the level of selfhood and cultural identities, how they are embedded in interpersonal relationships, and how they are shaped by, and shape, broader social processes.

Titles in the series:

Religion and Everyday Life
STEPHEN HUNT (2005)

Culture and Everyday Life
DAVID INGLIS (2005)

Community and Everyday Life
GRAHAM DAY (2005)

Consumption and Everyday Life
MARK W.D. PATERSON (2005)

Ethnicity and Everyday Life
CHRISTIAN KARNER (2007)

Globalization and Everyday Life
LARRY RAY (2007)

Gender and Everyday Life
MARY HOLMES (2008)

Self-Identity and Everyday Life
HARVIE FERGUSON (2009)

Risk, Vulnerability and Everyday Life
IAIN WILKINSON (2009)

Forthcoming titles in the series:

Cities and Everyday Life
DAVID PARKER (2009)

Nationalism and Everyday Life
JANE HINDLEY (2009)

The Body and Everyday Life
HELEN THOMAS (2009)

Media and Everyday Life
ELLIS CASHMORE (2009)

RISK, VULNERABILITY AND EVERYDAY LIFE

IAIN WILKINSON

Routledge
Taylor & Francis Group

LONDON AND NEW YORK

First published 2010 by Routledge
2 Park Square, Milton Park, Abingdon, Oxon, OX14 4RN

Simultaneously published in the USA and Canada
by Routledge
270 Madison Avenue, New York, NY 10016

*Routledge is an imprint of the Taylor & Francis Group,
an informa business*

© 2010 Iain Wilkinson

Typeset in Garamond and Scala by
Swales & Willis Ltd, Exeter, Devon
Printed and bound in Great Britain by
TJ International Ltd, Padstow, Cornwall

British Library Cataloguing in Publication Data
A catalogue record for this book is available from the British Library

Library of Congress Cataloging in Publication Data
Wilkinson, Iain, 1969–
Risk, vulnerability and everyday life / Iain Wilkinson.
p. cm. — (New Sociology)
Includes bibliographical references and index.
1. Risk—Sociological aspects. I. Title.
HM1101.W553 2009
302'.12—dc22
2008055158

ISBN 10: 0–415–37079–5 (hbk)
ISBN 10: 0–415–37080–9 (pbk)
ISBN 10: 0–203–03058–3 (ebk)

ISBN 13: 978–0–415–37079–0 (hbk)
ISBN 13: 978–0–415–37080–6 (pbk)
ISBN 13: 978–0–203–03058–5 (ebk)

CONTENTS

SERIES EDITOR'S FOREWORD

'The New Sociology' is a Series that takes its cue from massive social transformations currently sweeping the globe. Globalization, new information technologies, the techno-industrialization of warfare and terrorism, the privatization of public resources, the dominance of consumerist values: these developments involve major change to the ways people live their personal and social lives today. Moreover, such developments impact considerably on the tasks of sociology, and the social sciences more generally. Yet, for the most part, the ways in which global institutional transformations are influencing the subject-matter and focus of sociology have been discussed only in the more advanced, specialized literature of the discipline. I was prompted to develop this Series, therefore, in order to introduce students – as well as general readers who are seeking to come to terms with the practical circumstances of their daily lives – to the various ways in which sociology reflects the transformed conditions and axes of our globalizing world.

Perhaps the central claim of the Series is that sociology is fundamentally linked to the practical and moral concerns of everyday life. The authors in this Series – examining topics all the way from the body to globalization, from self-identity to consumption – seek to demonstrate the complex, contradictory ways in which sociology is a necessary and very practical aspect of our personal and public lives. From one angle, this may seem uncontroversial. After all, many classical sociological analysts as well as those associated with the classics of social theory emphasized the practical basis of human knowledge, notably Emile Durkheim, Karl Marx, Max Weber, Sigmund Freud, and George Simmel, among many others. And yet there are major respects in which the professionalization of academic sociology during the latter period of the twentieth century led to a retreat from the everyday issues and moral basis of sociology itself. (For an excellent discussion of the changing relations between practical and professional sociologies see Charles Lemert, *Sociology After the Crisis*, Second Edition, Boulder: Paradigm, 2004.) As worrying as such a retreat from the practical and moral grounds of the discipline is, one of the main consequences of recent global transformations in the field of sociology has been a renewed emphasis on the mediation of everyday events and experiences by distant social forces, the intermeshing of the local and global in the production of social practices, and on ethics and moral responsibility at both the individual and collective levels. 'The New Sociology' Series traces out these concerns across the terrain of various themes and thematics, situating everyday social practices in the broader context of life in a globalizing world.

The notions of *risk* and *vulnerability* are especially relevant against this backdrop. Rich, hi-tech, polished societies across the world today appear to be in the grip of a collective disorder driven by risk. From the vulnerabilities of job insecurity to the risks of terrorism, it's official: risk has become one of the central drivers – and arguably *the* central driver – of the global economy. According to the widely acclaimed German social theorist Ulrich Beck, we now live in the era of 'world risk society'. The rise of societal risk, contends Beck, is bound up with the new electronic global economy – a world in which we live on the edge of high technological innovation and scientific development, but where no one fully understands the possible global risks and dangers we face. For Beck, and the countless sociologists influenced by his work, world risk society makes us both increasingly involved and vulnerable to local, national and global risks that we run in our personal and professional lives. The paradox of risk society, however, is that talk of risk brings with it new anxieties, uncertainties and insecurities. Perhaps this has something to do with the sheer scale – indeed, the magnitude – of global risk today. For as Iain Wilkinson underscores, in this detailed introductory overview *Risk, Vulnerability and Everyday Life*, we all face risks today that are socially, spatially and morally different in order and in consequence to those faced by previous generations. In this reflective, disturbing appraisal of the key theoretical and political disputes over risk in sociology, Wilkinson maps the import of both classical and contemporary social theories for the analysis of risk.

The psychological effects of living with globalized risk in our increasingly troubled and troubling times bring on high levels of vulnerability, uncertainty and anxiety. Divorce rates rising, marriage rates falling, mental health problems soaring, widespread political apathy and disengagement from public life: these are just some of the better known, and endlessly media-debated, symptoms arising in an age of intensive risk. Against this backcloth, Wilkinson sets out a grim and certainly worrying story about our openness to the world – as contemporary women and men seek to escape from their own ignorance into either flawed enlightenment or anything-goes relativism. Perhaps no one has captured the key dilemma of risk society better than Beck: prior to the advent of global risk, he notes, hazards 'assaulted the nose or the eyes and were thus perceptible to the senses, while the risks of civilization today typically escape perception' (Ulrich Beck, *Risk Society*, London: Sage, 1992, p. 21). Is it any wonder that, for many people, society is now the central source of anxiety, arousing fear of the unknown, the unexpected, and the unforeseen? Potential responses to such a world veer from silence and escapism to the playing down of risks to more careful, considerate ways of assessing risk possibilities, problems and perils. In this context, Wilkinson raises an important challenge to sociology: what will our response to the hybrid, pluralized, cosmopolitan future actually comprise?

Taking a hard look at the great global risks of the contemporary era, Wilkinson develops the twin strategy of reviewing social theories of risk and appraising the impacts of risk upon people's attitudes, behaviours and social practices. Of the former, he covers a very wide ground for the beginning student, ranging over the seminal contributions of not only Beck but Anthony Giddens, Zygmunt Bauman, Mary Douglas as well as Foucauldian-inspired approaches to risk. These are not simply rehearsals of modern social theory, but rather *encounters* whereby the reader will likely feel altered by the particular social-theoretical perspective under review. Perhaps even more challenging is Wilkinson's microscopic interrogation of risk-analysis, risk-detection and risk-minimization strategies operating within the spheres of government and social policy. Throughout his self-declared aim is to 'remind readers that they should always be working to identify the political values and ethical standpoints that moderate the ways in which the language of risk is used to depict social life'. Notice Wilkinson's own language: 'always be working ...'. Life in conditions of intensive risk society, as Wilkinson deftly shows, is one of active self-monitoring, self-governance, self-regulation and self-dramatization within the wider socio-economic fields of risk. We are all, whether we know it or not, half-consciously or reflex-like, 'always working' on the risks we navigate, calculate and undertake. In the end, *Risk, Vulnerability and Everyday Life* displays all the elements of a slow-burning thriller: I won't give the plot away here, but to say that Wilkinson's sociological recounting of risk rightly broadens the discussion to catastrophic social change and global political shock. In the aftermath of 9/11, the war of terror and newly emerging political issues of water security and climate change, this is exactly how the sociology of risk, vulnerability and everyday life should be pitched.

Anthony Elliott
Adelaide, 2009

1

SOCIOLOGY IN A WORLD OF RISK

The majority of people in industrially advanced nations are better fed, more affluent and living longer than at any other time in history. In addition to this, most are privileged to have access to the educational and technical resources to experience a range of material, cultural and symbolic goods that were entirely unknown to previous generations. On these grounds, one might well argue that we are living at the highpoint of modern civilisation. Yet at the same time, large numbers of people report that they feel dissatisfied with their lives. The great advancements that have taken place in industry, science and technology, and radical improvements in material conditions of life, do not appear to be matched by an increase in the amount of happiness. Indeed, there is a considerable amount of evidence to suggest that many are disposed to experience social conditions of modernity in terms of an anguished sense of homelessness and discontent. The World Health Organisation now ranks unipolar depressive disorders as the leading burden of disease in high-income countries (WHO 2001). In the UK it is calculated that 16.4 per cent of the adult population are afflicted with some kind of neurotic disorder (ONS 2002), while in the USA it is estimated that as many as 17.1 per cent are suffering from depression (Greden 2001).

The social causes of these discontents are well documented. We know a great deal about the structural conditions, social circumstances and events that are liable to make people feel deeply unhappy about their lives (Wilkinson 2001). Social researchers in the more 'advanced' industrial societies have repeatedly highlighted the ways in which conditions of work and employment in capitalist societies arouse a great deal of frustration and distress. There is a long tradition of research into the ways in which competitive individualism is bound to promote a spirit of restlessness and cold indifference in the conduct of day-to-day life, and where large numbers of people are committed to forging a sense of worth and identity through paid employment, then it is widely recognised that the social meaning of work is liable to be a source of considerable amounts of status anxiety (Fromm 1956; Marmot and Wilkinson 1999). Difficulties at work are also known to contribute to the breakdown of family relations, separation and divorce. Many studies point to the ways in which people suffer with the day-to-day stress involved in maintaining ties of family life and relationships of emotional dependency under conditions of job insecurity and flexible terms of employment (Borrell et al. 2004; Noble 2007; Russell et al. 2008; Therborn 2007).

The primary social indicators of distress such as rates of suicide, alcohol and drug addiction, rates of psychiatric morbidity and rates of disabling disease suggest that, whilst there are significant gender variables in people's expressions of unhappiness and coping behaviours, social-economic class is the major determinant of a person's well-being (Chandola 2000; Graham 2000; Kunst et al. 1998; Leyland 2004; Petrou et al. 2006; Power et al. 2005). Generally speaking, lower-income groups are liable to experience a higher frequency of distressing life events, are poorly resourced with the means to cope under conditions of adversity, display more symptoms of mental illness, suffer higher rates of chronic disease and die younger than higher income groups. In recent years, a considerable amount of attention has also been devoted to the bearing of age upon these factors. Whilst many problems of work and family life are experienced most intensively among young adults, rates of psychiatric morbidity among older sections of population are often linked to experiences of chronic pain associated with diseases of old age (WHO 2001: 8). Studies suggest that at any one time, between 10 per cent and 30 per cent of the population of the United States of American are suffering from disabling experiences of back pain, arthritis and migraine headaches, while in the United Kingdom it is estimated that this figure may be as a high as 46 per cent (Elliott et al. 1999; Gureje et al. 1998; Harris and Associates 1999; Koestler and Myers 2002).

In the opinion of many cultural commentators, the social aetiology of our discontents is also comprised by more diffuse experiences of anxiety that derive from the knowledge gathered through mass media of wars in distant lands, the burgeoning environmental crisis, multiple threats to our health and security and the hazards courted through scientific experiment and technological innovation (Giddens 1991; Elliott and Lemert 2006; Bauman 2006). It is argued that, whilst interacting with 'mediatised' flows of information about a world of imminent danger and impending cata-strophe, the populations of modern societies are bound to experience a heightened sense of existential anxiety with regard to their social purpose, culture identity and future prospects. Some even claim that the novelty and force of this experience is such that we are witness to the develop-ment of a culture and politics that is overwhelmingly preoccupied with manipulating and managing our collective imagination for disaster (Furedi 2006; Massumi 1993).

When placing all this in context, we should not forget that most social research that finds its way to publication is devoted to documenting the minority experience of the globe. Sociological narratives on modernity tend to subscribe to a highly myopic account of the prevailing experience of culture, economy and society; one redolent with the interests of liber-ally minded metropolitan elites in the most industrially and technologi-cally advanced sectors of the world. The history of social science has been overwhelmingly preoccupied with segments of the lives of the 15 per cent of people living in the richest enclaves of global capitalist society, and in these terms, can only be regarded as a highly partial, and somewhat naïve, account of the human costs and benefits of modernisation. Certainly, it appears to this writer that Western sociologists are all too inclined to neglect the brute fact that the vast majority of the world's population have never been party to the material affluence, health gains and hyper con-sumerism afforded by present conditions of modernity; or rather, con-sider this to be no more than a matter for passing comment or a topic that is best confined to the specialist field of 'development'.

For the majority of the 85 per cent of the world's population living in developing societies, everyday life consists in a bitter struggle for exis-tence under conditions where a combination of hard physical labour, mal-nutrition and disease are always threatening to bring their lives to a premature end. Arguably, it is the case that for these people, the history of modernity amounts to no more than an apocalypse of annihilation. Almost half of the world's population live on less than $2 dollars a day, while a fifth live in absolute poverty on less than $1 dollar a day. The life expectancy of a child born in sub-Saharan Africa is less than half for that of a child born in the United States (World Bank 2006). In developing societies, a third of all children suffer from malnutrition and it is estimated that 30,000 die each day from preventable causes (UNDP 2000/2001; UNDP 2003). Whilst those living in the richest parts of the globe now commonly die from so-called diseases of affluence, in developing societies 21 per cent of all deaths and 70 per cent of childhood deaths are caused by pneumonia, diarrhoea, malaria, measles and malnutrition (WHO 1999). The vulnerability of the poorest populations to such diseases is understood to be largely attributable to the fact that 1.1 billion people lack access to safe drinking water and 2.6 billion lack adequate sanitation facilities; indeed, this is the primary cause of death for the 1.8 million children that die from diarrhoea each year (4,900 each day) (UNDP 2006).

Sections of the populations of Western societies may now be worried by news reports on the possible effects of global warming on society and might be expressing some anxieties about the depletion of natural resources, but it appears that these factors are set to have a far more disruptive impact upon the livelihoods of the poor majorities of the world. Most environmental experts believe that we are already living amidst a global ecological catastrophe where the poorest countries of the world are bound to suffer ever more severe shortages of water and food. While it is already the case that around one billion people worldwide are suffering from malnutrition, the World Bank warns that food production will have to double over the next thirty-five years if we are not to avoid famine on a scale without historical precedent (UNFPA 2001). Moreover, when detailing the greatest threats to the future of humanity, it is the scarcity of water that is set to have some of the most catastrophic impacts upon people's health and safety (Alcamo et al. 2000). In many developing societies, rapid urbanisation is expected to increase dramatically the stress on diminishing water supplies and it is feared that rights to ownership and of control water will soon become a major source of conflict within and between nations. Indeed, this is already the case in the Occupied Palestinian Territories and in the Sahel region of Africa.

We are living in the most extraordinary period of world history; an age of profound differences and unparalleled extremes. In terms of the numbers privileged to participate in the material abundance and cultural riches afforded by conditions of modernity, then, certainly, this may be designated 'the best of times'. Yet at the same time, for the great many that are forced to live under conditions of extreme austerity, it is most definitely the worst. The last forty years are distinguished as a period in which social scientists, medical demographers and government statisticians have collected an unprecedented amount of data to formally document and systematically categorise the health and well-being of our global society. In 'objective' terms of measurement, more of us are healthier and wealthier than at any other time in living memory, but at the same time, we are living through the most socially divided period of history for which we have record. It is extremely doubtful whether the majority experience of global society provides grounds for human flourishing; rather, the brute fact is that the available metrics on human suffering point to a world in turmoil, with hundreds of millions of people being forced to exist in woefully deprived circumstances that fall a long way short of any humane standards of living.

Arguably, these are the conditions under which the quest for sociological enlightenment should be pursued with the utmost urgency. Modern ideals of human 'progress' have all too readily been made to appear redundant in face of the harsh realities of the worlds in which people are made to live, and this more than any other factor has served as the creative spur for foundational projects of social science. Some of the most celebrated texts in Western social science are inspired by the moral calamity of societies organised so as to leave large sections of population vulnerable to experience injustice, injury or harm.

Yet, on many accounts, such sensibilities hold no prominent place within the contemporary scene. At a point in history where, more than ever before, one might expect sociologists to be devoting their energies to large-scale projects of progressive social reform, it appears that most are inclined to shy away from this endeavour. In recent years, an unprecedented number of publications have been devoted to analysing the ways in which sociology appears to be suffering from a dearth of creative inspiration and political ambition. It has become commonplace to represent the discipline as mired in a state of 'crisis' (Horowitz 1993; Lemert 1995; Levine 1995; Mouzelis 1995; Savage and Burrows 2007; Schilling and Mellor 2001; Seidman 1994; Turner and Rojek 2001).

Karl Marx once wrote that 'the tradition of all dead generations weighs like a nightmare on the brain of living' (Marx [1851] 1977: 300), and it may now be the case that as a result of a greater consciousness of the human costs of modernisation and disastrous failings of previous world-changing movements, that the majority are reluctant to identify their vocation in terms of the pursuit of substantive social change. Certainly, most agree that if sociology has lost its ambition, then, particularly in the aftermath of the collapse of Soviet-style communism, this is in part a result of a widespread disillusionment with left-wing politics and a loss of faith in the ambitions of Western Marxism. At the same time, it is argued that in the act of distancing itself from Marxism, the discipline has abandoned many long-standing tools of analysis and critique so that it is now harder than ever to bring a coherent frame of sociological understanding to bear upon the world (Burawoy 2000, 2003; Lash and Urry 1987, 1994; Outhwaite and Ray 2005).

In some quarters, it is claimed that a great deal of sociological writing now presents us with no more than a 'zombified' account of the presiding experience of life in modern societies (Beck 2000a; Gane and Beck 2004). Concepts such as 'class', 'family' and 'nation state' are held to belong to a bygone age and we are urged to jettison these on the grounds that they no longer possess the descriptive or explanatory power to make known the social dynamics of our lives. On this account, a great deal of the language of sociology is analytically moribund; too much within our cultural experience and social behaviours now lies beyond its grasp. Where the sociological imagination was once celebrated for its capacity to make clear the interplay between history, self and social circumstance, it is now represented as a quality of mind that, while labouring under the burden of its history, struggles to make known its object of study and more often than not fails to deliver on its promise.

A number of prominent social theorists now openly admit to be working from the premise that the demands of our day require us to embark upon a major revision of our conceptual vocabulary and frameworks of analysis (Elliott 2003; Gane 2004). It is argued that intensifying global networks of social interaction require us to develop new ways of thinking about the dominant modes of cultural consciousness, political affiliation and social belonging that distinguish our times. Moreover, rapid scientific advancements within the field of genetics and a burgeoning knowledge of the ecological crisis are understood to announce a paradigm shift in the ethics of everyday life that requires a thorough reappraisal of traditional notions of 'citizenship rights' and 'civic virtue'. In essence, it is claimed that for sociology to be established as a discipline relevant for understanding the problems and experiences of twenty-first-century society, then it must create a new language of analysis and critique.

THE CONTEXT OF RISK

This book offers an introductory overview and critical contribution to a series of debates concerning the ways in which problems and experiences of risk are identified as the signature tune of our times. Whilst it may be conceded that a focus on shared experiences and expressions of risk provides insights into the distinctive character of contemporary social life, some go so far as to suggest that 'risk' is now the organising principle of society as well as the overriding preoccupation of our political culture and a major co-ordinate of personal identity. A group of influential social theorists advance the study of risk as a core component of the vanguard of a new sociological reformation (Beck 1992, 1999; Giddens 1990; Bauman 2003: 186–222). This understanding also leads many more to designate the analysis of 'risk consciousness' and contrasting modes of 'risk discourse' as among the most important considerations in a serious attempt to frame modern life with sociological meaning. The field of risk research has been developed to a point where it is possible to devote an entire career to analysing the bearing of distinct components of risk upon people's attitudes, and behaviours. Risk in social science commands the attentions of at least four specialist journals and is regularly taken up as a headline topic of interest in special editions of mainstream publications. A range of undergraduate textbooks now identify the interrelationship between risk and society as among the most pressing of contemporary concerns (Adams 1995; Boyne 2003; Denney 2005; Lupton 1999).

There is already a vast amount of empirical research and theoretical writing that is dedicated to the study of risk. There is no agreement, however, as to how risk should be defined and studied, and certainly there is no consensus when it comes to identifying the social conditions and cultural dispositions that are implicated within the rise of risk debate in the public sphere. A major problem for any introduction to the sociology of risk lies in the task of equipping students with the analytical tools to make sense of the many contrasting ways in which the language of risk features as a label for social problems and as a means to interpret people's thoughts and behaviours.

As a point of entry into this arena, I hold that it is worth distinguishing between the adoption of the concept of risk as a component of cultural narratives about society and the ways in which it features as an analytical term within the designation of social attitudes and behaviours. In the former, problems of risk are raised as a means to address the sociological and/or cultural meaning of emergent social trends or general conditions of social life, while in the latter, the issue of risk features as part of the effort to understand the specific ways in which people perceive and respond to a host of hazards and conditions of threatening uncertainty. There are some interests that are shared across these fields, but it is generally the case that while cultural narratives about risk are comprised by broad ranging commentaries on the socio-cultural dynamics of our times, sociological engagements with facets of risk analysis tend to be more involved with an inter-disciplinary policy domain engaged with the regulatory apparatus designed for managing the health and safety of populations.

In social theory, writing about risk in contemporary society is often taken as an opportunity to expand upon the cultural meaning and political significance of institutional developments and social practices that involve a great deal more than risk per se. The focus on risk serves as an entry point into long-standing sociological debates over the course of processes of rationalisation, the fate of Western democracy, new class alignments, social forces of individualisation, the social implications of the burgeoning environmental crisis and the presiding cultural character of modern life. The concept of risk is used as a heuristic device that is tailored to lend support to distinct traditions of theorising the relationship between the individual and society. Writers such as Niklas Luhmann, Ulrich Beck, Mary Douglas, Anthony Giddens and Nikolas Rose give privileged space to the concept risk with their social theories, but each works with a different theoretical agenda in mind. Here the task of evaluating issues of risk requires students to work at understanding its location within distinct, and sometimes opposing, styles of sociological thinking. In order to appreciate the interests and values at stake, they must be prepared to investigate the sociological foundations on which writers promote their favoured representations of society and advance opposing accounts of the cultural experience of individuals within this.

When it comes to making sense of the involvement of sociology within the field of risk analysis, then it is important to recognise the extent to which this tends to be dominated by an interest in understanding people's aptitudes for probabilistic thinking. Whilst at the level of popular understanding and cultural commentary the concept of risk tends to be used as a synonym for 'danger' or 'hazardous uncertainty', the field of risk analysis generally operates with a stricter and more traditional under-standing of risk – a mode of thinking in which the costs and benefits of specific actions and discrete events are weighed in the balance. A man-agerial ethos often exerts a heavy influence over the topics that are priori-tised for research; in this regard, it appears that when it comes to the effective organisation of society, a popular assumption holds that this is best achieved through the shaping and disciplining of people's attitudes and opinions. Cognitive psychology, and particularly that which places a high value on psychometric testing as the means to reveal individual thought processes and motivations, tends to set the agenda for this work. In this context, sociologists either assume the role of providing a 'social' supplement to psychology or present themselves as offering a critical challenge to the ways in which this kind of research takes place. Here the assessment of risk debates in social science rests on an acquaintance with the conceptual premises, methodological preferences and institutional histories that distinguish psychology from sociology. It involves an ability to question the ways in which research problems are identified and a capacity to recognise the values and interests that are privileged within contrasting practices of data collection and analysis.

Throughout my writing I have tried to make clear the contexts of risk debate to which my terms of analysis are addressed. In what follows, I fre-quently remind readers that they should always be working to identify the political values and ethical standpoints that moderate the ways in which the language of risk is used to depict social life. I aim to expose the poten-tial for forms of political and cultural bias to shape the ways in which risk analysis is brought to the task of categorising individual thoughts and actions. From the outset I take the view that we should be wary of any instance where the concept of risk features without any prior qualification as a label for 'social problems' or as a means to refer to 'common-sense' attitudes and 'ordinary' behaviours. There are always political and moral interests at stake in the forms of language that we favour as a means to represent the social world. Both at the level of public debate and in the more academically refined realms of sociological discourse, it is often the case that concepts are privileged because of their ideological appeal. The semantic currency of symbolic forms of representation is always liable to change and there are many occasions where this is moderated in relation to the exercise of power in society. I hold that this is particularly the case with regard to the language of risk and throughout my writing I aim to be attentive to this matter.

AIMS AND OBJECTIVES

My interest lies in exploring the ways in which problems of risk have not only been established as objects of sociological research, but also have begun to shape the language of sociological theory and logics of research practice. Accordingly, whilst outlining sociological explanations for the rise of popular interest in issues of risk, I am also concerned to inquire into what a preoccupation with risk does to sociology. At the same time as I take seriously the suggestion that people's attitudes and behaviours are increasingly animated by thoughts about risk, I also stand at a critical distance from this claim so as to reflect upon the extent to which it promotes a partial account of lived experience that is also subject to the play of ideology. In so doing, I advocate an approach to study that at the same time as it applies the tools of sociology to understanding our world also works to nurture a critical reflexivity towards the cultural values and methodological practices by which it produces its knowledge and judges its worth. I have approached the task of writing with the aim of balancing an introductory account of the sociology of risk with a critical investigation of the ways in which the study of risk serves to discipline the character of sociology. I am not only concerned to reflect on what is sociologically at stake in the depiction of our world as a 'risk society', but I am also interested to make clear the conceptual premises, ethical leanings and political orientations of the kinds of sociology that embrace this theme. I will be asking the question: what happens to the sociological imagination when the concept of risk is privileged as a core unit of analysis and made part of the language of critique?

In the chapter that follows, I outline some key junctures in the semantic history of risk. This is for the purpose of equipping readers with insights into the social, cultural and political conditions that are responsible for making risk a pressing matter of sociological concern. I argue that shifts in the meaning of risk are rooted in the history of modern processes of rationalisation. In order to help students appreciate the importance of the association between risk and rationalisation, I dwell upon the ways in which the early development of modern administrative practices and techniques of insurance led to the adoption of the category of risk as a means to represent calculations of uncertainty. I also examine some of the ways in which techniques of risk assessment were incorporated within the logics and ethos of modern social policy and public health administration. Insofar as it is now the case that many social conflicts surround definitions of risk and techniques of risk assessment, I contend that this reflects the increasing amounts of moral and political concern that are directed towards the intensifying force of rationalisation upon our lives as well as the many unintended consequences of this process. The politicisation of risk is at the same time a politicisation of techniques and tendencies of rationalisation. It is generally the case that public debates about risk involve disputes over the ways in which new technologies of rationalisation are applied to the management of health, industry, occupational behaviours, welfare services, governmental administration, safety regulations and the natural environment.

Whilst underlining the extent to which the language of risk and techniques of risk assessment are wedded to processes of rationalisation, I argue that Max Weber, the social theorist who has done more than any other to explain the peculiar cultural character of modern rationality and its social consequences, still has a great deal to teach us about the contemporary preoccupation with risk. One of the more innovative features of my overview of the sociology of risk concerns the potential for a Weberian frame of analysis to be brought to bear upon the ways in which problems of risk are culturally represented and treated as pressing matters of social concern. This is first raised for consideration in Chapter 2 but also features in later sections where I dwell more directly upon the dangers posed by the risk paradigm to sociology.

In Chapter 3, I present an introductory overview of the social theories that have exerted an influence over the ways in which the topic of risk has been incorporated within the field of sociology. I highlight the extent to which, in marked contrast to expert/managerial concern with shaping people's aptitudes for probabilistic thinking, social theorists tend to be interested in ways in which disputes about risk are linked to the play of ideology and the exercise of social power. Whilst dwelling on the distinctive attributes of the frameworks proposed by Ulrich Beck, Mary Douglas and Foucauldian theorists of 'governmentality' for the analysis of risk, I also note the political interests that appear to discipline the ways they interpret the social meaning of this phenomenon and its ramifications for the dynamics of social and cultural change.

Chapter 4 examines the forms of empirical research that have been brought to the task of establishing how people interpret and respond to risk in everyday life. I treat this as a platform on which to raise critical questions about the evidence base on which theoretical claims are advanced. I also approach this as an opportunity to highlight some of the distinguishing attributes of a sociological approach to empirical research as opposed to that which takes place under the auspices of psychology. I focus on the ways in which sociological attempts to locate the meaning of risk in social context have a tendency to raise more wide-ranging debates about the techniques of data collection and analysis that are privileged as a means to reveal 'the truth' about human outlooks and behaviours. I argue for the value of a reflexive sociology that works to make clear the limits of its knowledge claims and the contingencies of the social practices involved in their creation. I also note the propensity of such a perspective to cast social science in a moral and political frame so that conceptual tools, measuring techniques and analytical practices are assessed in terms of their sectional biases and ideological appeal.

In Chapter 5, I provide a more sustained sociological critique of ways in which the study of risk has been incorporated within contemporary social science. In this I aim to make clear some of the limits that are set upon the sociological imagination when the concept of risk is privileged as a means to analyse people's attitudes and behaviours. I also aim to expose the ways in which the priorities set for contemporary risk research are liable to involve sociologists in addressing problems that, at best, only involve the interests and experiences of tiny sections of more privileged sectors of society. In particular, I dwell upon the extent to which current agendas of debate within the sociology of risk and risk research appear to be largely detached from any concern to establish the social distribution of harm within and between societies. In the final analysis, I argue that if one holds to the belief that sociology should be particularly attentive to the human costs of modernisation and that it should serve as a means to promote values of social justice, then it is doubtful that such convictions will be adequately accommodated within the parameters of risk debate.

In the final chapter I outline the contours of the *new* world risk society that has rapidly taken shape as crises in financial markets, coupled with volatilities in energy supplies and global food shortages have begun to feature as ever-present concerns in everyday life. I suggest that such matters will lead to a radical reappraisal of the priorities set for risk research and that it may already be the case that a great deal of the risk debate in contemporary social science has been superseded by the magnitude of the problems raised through these recent shocks to the globe. I refer to a range of government reports and policy documents where the consensus holds that world society has already entered a new era of catastrophe that will be marked both by intensifying struggles for resources to meet basic human needs and by unprecedented strains on civil society. I conclude with a statement on the new sociology that could emerge from this point and the type of sociological calling with which we might live towards the possible futures that await us.

2

THE HISTORY OF RISK

Raymond Williams notes that periods of social upheaval give rise to new idioms of cultural expression (Williams 1976). He argues that the introduction of new words into our language tends to take place where people experience major transformations in their material conditions of existence, political expectations and cultural outlooks. It appears that when immersed in processes of social and cultural change, we are driven by shifts in circumstance to create symbolic forms of culture for reinterpreting the day-to-day meaning of our lives. Where it is possible to associate a particular word with a competing range of meanings or pronounced conflicts of interpretation, then Williams suggests that we should take this as a sign that something important is at stake; semantic disputes usually take place in areas of life where there is much to be lost or gained. He urges us to approach such occasions as an opportunity for gathering insights into the cultural ideals, social values and political aspirations that people hold most dear.

This chapter is written with the understanding that the concept of risk can be studied in these terms. I hold to the view that the different ways in which the concept of risk is mobilised as a means to label social problems, describe common states of mind, delineate new domains of social policy and define political objectives, amounts to an opportunity for broadening our understanding of the distinctive cultural character and social psychology of our times. On these grounds I contend that in so far as social researchers fail to attend to conflicting interpretations of risk and see no reason to declare their preferred account of the meaning of this concept, then they are also failing to think critically about their choice of language and research practice. The language of risk is imbued with philosophical conviction, moral preference and ideological commitment and if we are to be serious in our search for knowledge of society, then we should work at sensitising ourselves to all that is implied in the adoption of this term as a common unit of description and analysis.

The original meaning of risk is rooted in the development of calculative reason and is used with reference to the prospect of acquisitive opportunity. This positive account of risk is still to be found in the world of business management and commerce; indeed, financial markets thrive on the trading of risk. The meaning of risk as calculative, opportunistic and acquisitive might also be associated with sporting and leisure pursuits that involve a controlled brush with the thrill of danger. However, now it is arguably the case that such positive appreciations of risk are confined to a minority; for at the level of popular understanding, it appears this word is more often used to highlight the prospect of imminent danger and harm. For many, the concept of risk now has wholly negative connotations. Indeed, in current sociology it is generally assumed that the study of risk concerns debates over the reality of dangers facing society, the task of managing threats to people's well-being and security and attempts to map the ways in which individuals think, feel and act when they acquire knowledge about hazards. In modern times, the concept of risk is most often used to bring emphasis to domains of threatening uncertainty.

When it comes to the task of writing about risk, our frameworks of analysis will be co-ordinated by the ways in which we choose to explain these shifts in meaning and emphasis. In contemporary sociology this is the hermeneutical terrain upon which characterisations of our culture, society and politics are advanced within favoured narratives on modernity, and in many cases, these present us with conflicting moral and sociological judgements on the overall direction of change. The cultural prominence of risk has been interpreted either as a sign that society is losing faith in the ideals of Enlightenment, or conversely, as support for the view that we are presented with new opportunities for advancing an enhanced vision of enlightened society. Whilst some claim that the widespread use of the language of risk reveals the extent to which threatening uncertainties mark the everyday experience of life, others regard this more as a manifestation of forms of culture and society that are highly regulated via intensifying forces of technological control. Where the labelling of social problems in terms of risk may be taken as grounds for claiming that people are prone to irrational displays of anxiety, on other accounts, it is understood to mean that anxieties are being allayed through a process of rational planning and administrative intervention. Debates on risk in the public sphere are identified with political decisions that curtail personal freedoms so as to advance authoritarian measures of social control, but may also be represented as the vanguard of movements of democratic reform.

The reasons behind these conflicts of interpretation are not always made clear. Indeed, many pay no heed to the extent to which their professed points of view are held in tension with many counter opinions and opposing renditions of the state we are in (or moving away from). For the most part, writers do not appear to be particularly concerned to identify the point where political preference, institutional bias or personal conviction begin to shape their accounts of what risk means for society. Social commentators may draw critical attention to the unequal power relations that appear to moderate the ways in which the language of risk is used in the public sphere, but they seldom venture to declare the ideological bearings of their own approach to research.

In what follows, I aim to sensitise readers to the ways in which the concept of risk serves as the means to frame social processes and critical events with historical, political and moral meaning. The first section outlines key junctures in the semantic history of risk and highlights the ways in which these take place in response to wider processes of social, economic, political and technological change. In the second section I argue that it is by locating the history of risk as a component of modern processes of rationalisation that we uncover the analytical terrain on which to investigate its social and political significance. I suggest that Max Weber still has a great deal to teach us about the accumulated meanings of risk and the paradoxical ways in which the concept features in contemporary life both as a cue for social anxiety and cultural alarm and as an emblem of calculative reason and technological control. I offer an approach to studying risk that locates its meaning within established conventions of sociological analysis, but where I move to highlight some of the neglected themes within Max Weber's account of modern processes of rationalisation, I aim to shed light upon the political and moral ramifications of the labelling of social problems as 'risk'.

THE ACCUMULATED MEANINGS OF RISK

1 Calculation for acquisition

The etymology of the concept of risk is inconclusive but ultimately it may be derived from the Arabic word *risq*, which means riches or good fortune (Skeat 1910). However, where there is also an attempt to recover its origins in the Greek word *rhiza*, meaning cliff, and the Latin *resegare*, meaning 'to cut off short', John Ayto suggests that risk has its semantic roots embedded in a classical maritime vocabulary as a term invoking the perils of sailing too closely to inshore rocks (Ayto 1990). It is perhaps interesting to note that during the Middle Ages both of these possible meanings come together when the concept of risk is first adopted as a principle of maritime insurance. In this context, risk is used to refer to acquisitive ventures that court misfortune or flirt with catastrophe.

Florence Edler de Roover claims that it was during the Commercial Revolution (1275–1375) that Italian shipping merchants first began to use modern-style insurance contracts as a means to manage their business affairs (de Roover 1945). This period saw the emergence of a new type of business arrangement where, rather than travelling with their goods in order to secure a transaction, merchants could choose to stay at home and use a system of insurance loans as an incentive for shipowners to guarantee the safe delivery of their cargo. As merchants acquired the confidence to invest in the probability of a successful venture, then it became possible to transfer the whole burden of risk to an indirectly attached third party as in a formal premium insurance contract. The earliest recorded examples of premium insurance contracts were drawn up in Palermo in 1350; however, they may already have been in use before this date in the more important business centres of Florence and Pisa. Under the provisions of these contracts, the business relationship between the insurer and the insured was reversed for the first time. Under an earlier system of sea loans, the insured party was obliged on safe arrival of his goods to pay a sum of money, the large part of which he had already received. By contrast, under the arrangement of premium insurance, the insurer, having agreed on a premium, received nothing in advance and was now obliged to pay out a sum of money even if the business venture ended in disaster.

In the context of insurance, the concept of risk features as an abstract, transferable, symbolic representation of people's confidence in their ability to understand and manage the hazards of contingency (Ewald 1991).

At its origins the language of risk may be interpreted as a cultural expression of people's increased faith in abstract techniques of calculation and rational analysis. Where merchants begin to insure themselves against risk as a matter of effective business management, we can also take this as a sign of a growing acceptance of the rule of calculation as a means to predict the future.

The communication of probabilities in terms of risk occurs at the point where societies acquired a technological mastery over nature whereby it was possible to place a measure of guarantee on the likelihood that ships will sail safely across treacherous seas. Such guarantees could only be made when societies were ordered and controlled to a point where one could expect to travel great distances under the protection of the law and free from the threat of piracy. They required the maintenance of social order and institutional stability across wide tracts of time and space. They relied on the possibility that planning for the future could take place with reference to regular patterns of past events. From the twelfth century up to second half of the nineteenth century, the history of risk may be associated with an accentuated development in the understanding that natural and social worlds possess law-like properties that can be studied as the grounds for rational planning. In this regard, economic historian Peter Bernstein refers to risk as 'the revolutionary idea that defines the boundary between modern times and the past' (Bernstein 1998: 1).

2 The politics of uncertainty

A second major juncture in the semantic history of risk takes place during the nineteenth century when techniques of risk calculation are adapted for the purposes of controlling the spread of illness, levels of poverty and rates of crime. Taking their cue from the 'genealogical' writings of Michel Foucault (see Chapter 3), a number of commentators identify a major turning point in our understanding of risk to originate in the development of modern social policy. On this account, as modern nation states sought to develop a rational means to manage the social and economic dynamics of industrialisation, actuarial techniques of risk assessment were adapted for the purpose of making populations 'thinkable and measurable for the purposes of government' (Stenson 1998). Where up to this point calculations of risk were largely associated with individual acquisitive ventures, with the rise of the modern nation state, it is possible to identify a new risk 'mentality' at work within state policies designed to build more rational forms of society and welfare administration. Accordingly, the framing of social problems as 'risks for society', the identification of particular groups and individuals as 'risks to society' and the labelling of segments of population as 'at risk' are held to signal the emergence of social institutions, legal frameworks and expertise designed to protect and promote the nation's health, wealth and social well-being.

As far as Britain is concerned, Ian Hacking identifies 1820–40 as the period when an 'avalanche of numbers' first descended upon the ordering of human affairs (Hacking 1990, 1991). By the middle of the nineteenth century, statistical data on population trends had become an indispensable component of public debates over the ills of society. Indeed, among the 'moral scientists' of the day it was widely assumed that it was by techniques of enumeration and classification that one might be able to establish a means of imposing more effective measures of control upon the 'deviant' elements of a population (Hacking 1990: 3). The drive to discover the statistical laws governing human social behaviour took place under the auspices of a moral and political project to reduce rates of crime, suicide, vagrancy, prostitution and disease. It is at this time that, alongside concerns to identify dangerous classes that posed risks to civil society, we find policy debates arriving at a focus upon the 'at-risk child' and the emergence of regulatory frameworks for managing risks associated with the production of food (Draper and Green 2002; Lubeck and Garrett 1990; Parton 1998).

With the benefit of hindsight, the impact of these developments on the meaning of risk was twofold, and in both instances may be designated as unintended consequences of movements to apply actuarial techniques of risk analysis to ever more complex and expansive domains of social behaviour. The first (and earlier) shift in the meaning of risk served to accentuate the elements of *uncertainty* contained in measures of risk calculation. The second moved to frame the uncertainties of risk calculation as a matter for political debate. On this understanding, the politicisation of the language of risk is, in part, a consequence of the ways in which advanced actuarial techniques of risk assessment make clear the domains of uncertainty that comprise calculations of probability. The greater the knowledge of uncertainty, the more it becomes evident that disputes surrounding the accuracy of risk calculation (or rather, that disputes surrounding the probability that decisions based on risk calculation will have negative consequences for society) can only be settled by an exercise of institutional power and political will.

The more concerted the actuarial attempt to bring social behaviour under the rule of calculation, the more experts were alerted to indeterminate elements in people's social outlooks and behaviours. As techniques of classification became ever more nuanced and methods of statistical analysis grew in sophistication to the point where multiple social variables and social circumstances were included in calculations of future probabilities, the more it became possible to highlight points where leaps of prognostication are a *necessary* component of expert accounts of the reality of risk. The more ambitious the expert attempt to measure social risks, the more they were attuned to the domains of uncertainty included in their accounts of the possible futures that await us. Whilst on many occasions finding that their measurements were a reliable guide to predicting social behaviours, at the same time, experts became more alert than ever before to the extent to which social reality may well confound the rule of calculation.

As a result of the dramatic advances in techniques of calculation whereby increasing amounts of statistical information were gathered on the irreducibly complex and spontaneous elements in human behaviours that actuarial experts became more fully aware of the extent to which an 'ultimate indeterminism' lay behind the appearance of regularity in human affairs (Hacking 1991). Whilst at the beginning of the nineteenth century, social scientists might have reasonably assumed that social orders were determined by universal laws of nature which, in principle, were amenable to rational understanding, within the space of 100 years it was clear that chance events always contributed to the development of the social structures in which we are made to live. On these grounds, at the same time as Peter Bernstein celebrates the wisdom of hindsight afforded by modern techniques of risk assessment he also underlines the extent to which experts are more alert than most to the tentative and provisional nature of their conclusions (Bernstein 1998). With reference to advances in actuarial techniques for forecasting economic trends he argues that the greater the attempt to predict the future on the basis of risk calculation, the more we are bound to recognise that 'surprise is endemic' in our history, particularly in light of the knowledge we have gathered on the 'discontinuities, irregularities and volatilities' of human societies. Accordingly, Bernstein advises that we pay heed to the fact that economic and political decisions based on risk calculation, by necessity, include many subjective leaps of faith. At the same time as advanced techniques of risk assessment allow for rational planning on an unprecedented scale, they also increase our knowledge of the magnitude of indeterminacy which is contained in any attempt to predict the future.

For these reasons Bob Heyman and Mette Henriksen (1998) emphasise that assessment of risk is not so much a property of the world, but more a product of the way we construct our knowledge of the possible futures which await us. They hold that risk is a 'simplifying heuristic' for guiding action in face of the irreducible indeterminism of complex social processes (Heyman 1998: 5), and, further, they contend that this inevitably renders the language of risk open to being appropriated for ideological ends. They argue that in any debate over the reality of risk an accent can be placed on either the uncertainties or the certainties of risk calculation, and that it is in accordance with an individual's moral stance and political point of view that they tend to add emphasis to one side or the other.

Using examples drawn from the context of health care, Heyman and Henriksen note that whilst probability statements incorporating the language of risk are used to highlight the likelihood of positive outcomes from medical interventions, on other occasions, they feature as the means to draw social attention to hazards associated with particular procedures. In their study of the communication of probabilities in prenatal genetic counselling they found that:

> [A] woman may be told either that she has a probability of 1:100 of having a miscarriage through amniocentesis, or a probability of 99:100 of not suffering this adversity. Professionals may use the latter, more optimistic, descriptive device in order to encourage risk acceptance.
>
> (Heyman and Henriksen 1998: 28)

Elsewhere Heyman notes that applications for research funding made to his local medical ethics committee tend to lay particular emphasis upon the extent to which such quantitative probability estimates can give a false impression of the accuracy of statistical calculations of risk (ibid.: 76). Accordingly, researchers may highlight the extent to which assessments of risk can only be achieved at the expense of a reduced conception of the complexity in real systems of cause and effect, particularly where these concern the vagaries of human behaviour. As far as the calculation of health risks is concerned, it is not only the case that it is often impossible to specify the full range of variables which may contribute to the likelihood of an individual contracting a particular type of disease, but also that the ways in which people reflexively incorporate the knowledge of being labelled 'at risk' can be extremely unpredictable (ibid.: 71–80). Indeed, these writers place a particular emphasis upon the extent to which the unpredictability of patients' responses to being informed about risk can have both positive and negative outcomes as far as their long-term health is concerned (ibid.: 95–6); where some respond to the threat of danger by taking every precautionary measure to enhance their chances of maximising their health, others are inclined to adopt even more reckless forms of behaviour (ibid.: 71). Accordingly, the dissemination of knowledge about risk may actually diminish our capacity to predict the magnitude of its negative impact upon the ways in which a population experiences their health.

François Ewald underscores the political ramifications of this understanding of risk (Ewald 1991, 1993). He argues that it is because of advancements in modern societies' technological capacity for analysing social and economic processes in terms of risk that the acceptability of risk is bound to become a political preoccupation. He notes that where, on the one hand, governments and business corporations may refer to expert assessments of risk as a means to emphasise the extent to which the benefits of a particular technology far outweigh its costs and to convince 'the public' that every precautionary measure is in place so as to ensure their safety, on the other hand, some will seize upon the inevitable uncertainties of this knowledge so that where it remains possible to associate that technology with the (statistically remote) possibility of disaster, the risk will be deemed 'unacceptable'. Knowledge of risk may now be used on one side to highlight 'chance' and 'opportunity' and on the other to accentuate 'uncertainty' and 'danger'; where 'taking risks' in the spirit of enterprise tends to embrace its positive meaning, those that identify themselves as standing 'at risk' seek to draw attention to the potential for the future to visit us with danger. Indeed, Ewald claims that where as a matter of everyday language one is now most likely to encounter the term being used as another word for 'danger', this testifies to the extent to which, during the last century, the massive expansion of the 'technology of risk' has *itself* exacerbated people's anxieties over the hazards courted by modern industry and science.

3 The ideology of risk in everyday life

A further level of complexity is brought to the social meaning of risk when we examine the ways in which this concept now features as part of the language of everyday life. Here the word 'risk' is used as a synonym for 'danger', but without any reference being made to technical aspects of risk calculation. Generally speaking, when news media report on risks to society or when individuals talk about risks to themselves, they intend to refer us to the possible harms that may be done to ourselves and others. On most occasions, in everyday life the language of risk is used not so much as a cue to raise questions of mathematics, but more as a means to highlight common 'worries', 'problems' and 'concerns'.

Mary Douglas argues that we should understand this development as bearing testimony to the extent to which the majority of people in modern industrial societies hold calculative reason and scientific procedure in high regard. For Douglas, the fact that people prefer to talk about 'risks' rather than 'dangers' implies that they are seeking to underline the seriousness of their concerns with an oblique reference to the rationality of science (Douglas 1992). Douglas interprets the popularisation of the association of 'risk' with 'danger' as a sign of the extent to which people (at least by implication) recognise that their personal worries are much more likely to be perceived as legitimate when they appear to have science on their side (see Chapter 3). Accordingly, it may well be the case that a further unintended consequence of the rationalisation of our social life and moral conduct is a more widespread cultural appropriation of rational concepts such as 'risk' for popular causes, moral arguments and political contests that are only tangentially related (if at all) to disciplines of expert inquiry and scientific debate.

In Douglas's account this cultural appropriation of the language of risk illustrates the popular appeal of science within Western modernity. Where mention of risk is used to sound social alarms and is taken up by pressure groups as 'a stick to beat authority', then she tends to present this as a cultural shift that takes place 'from below' (Douglas 1992). The everyday meaning of 'risk' as 'danger' is explained as a lay response to the ways in which state authorities and large corporations are popularly perceived to threaten people's preferred 'ways of life'. She holds that in social contexts of heightened anxiety, modern individuals are prone to respond by complaining about being placed 'at risk', and this implies an effort to marshal the authority of science on behalf of their grievances (Douglas and Wildavsky 1982; Douglas 1986).

However, it is also important to recognise that this shift in the everyday currency of risk is at the same time encouraged 'from above'. Actuarial conceptions of risk may well feature as part of the language of expert debate, but when it comes to the task of persuading people to moderate their behaviours and attitudes in line with expert advice, it is now possible to find many instances where officials work at using the threat of danger coded as a 'risk' as a technique of social control. In recent years, a number of studies have been devoted to documenting the ways in which governments (especially in Britain, Australia and New Zealand) have incorporated the codification of 'danger' as 'risk' within documents relating to health policy, social welfare provision and criminal justice legislation (Culpitt 1999; Kemshall 2002; O'Malley 2004; Petersen and Wilkinson 2008). Attention is focused on the ways in which re-drafted health and safety regulations and government-sponsored tracts on various aspects of health promotion highlight 'risks' for individual and institutional attention. At this point, it appears that a more emotively laden conception of risk is deployed as a governmental strategy designed to encourage people to adopt precautionary measures to protect themselves and others from various types of harm.

A considerable amount of research is now devoted to studying the ways in which individuals and groups respond to the official labelling of aspects of their lifestyles and behaviours in terms of 'risk'. In this respect, the new inter-disciplinary field of 'risk analysis' is largely preoccupied with documenting the cultural frames of reference by which possible dangers are made known to society, and how in turn, different segments of society respond to government and/or corporate 'risk communication' campaigns. Where governments fund health promotion campaigns relating to risks associated with our eating habits, childhood, sexual behaviours, cigarette smoking and alcohol consumption, then studies have focused on the different ways in which individuals judge the severity of the threats they are faced with and the kinds of behaviours they are inclined to adopt in order to stay out of harms way. A great deal of attention has also come to rest upon the ways in which civil and commercial organisations, either in response to the incursion of new regulatory regimes upon their activities or under the effort to maintain and promote a positive reputation in public life, are made to manage an ever expanding portfolio of institutional risk (Power 2004).

In everyday life the concept of risk now features as a core component of popular languages of complaint. In official discourse and in news media, it is also deployed as a means to shape public opinion, individual behaviours and corporate cultures. While it may well be the case that it retains an aura of calculation and science, above all else, in these contexts the concept of risk is used as a means to sound social alarms. Once labelled as 'risk', problems are framed with a sense of urgency that issues a demand for political attention and moral response. Here the language of risk is always at the same time a discourse of power. The flagging of risks is ideologically motivated; it is geared to challenge opinions, promote interests and direct behaviour. From an analytical point of view, it can be framed as part of a cultural arsenal by which efforts are made to discipline social perceptions and behaviours so that these more readily conform to preferred renditions of what is 'reasonable' and 'proportional' in face of a particular worry or concern. Now it often appears that where reference is made to risk we also encounter movements for cultural and social change. Risk issues a demand for a change of cultural outlook and social conduct; it is a concept geared to exercise power.

RISK AND MODERN PROCESSES OF RATIONALISATION

In the preceding account of cultural shifts in the meaning of risk I have suggested that developments within the history of this concept are intimately connected to technologies, social contexts and political movements of *rationalisation*. There is a long tradition in Western sociology of identifying the rise of modern societies with cultural practices that advance instrumental reason as the most efficient and desirable means of dealing with the social and natural world. Accordingly, the modern worldview is held to be characterised by the understanding that the dynamics of nature and society are governed by law-like principles that can be made the objects of calculation, and, further, that these are a sufficient and reliable guide for social action and technological intervention. One of the defining characteristics of our times is manifest in the extent to which our personal conduct and institutional arrangements are made subject to a 'formal rationality' that aims to calculate the most efficient means to resolve problems by bringing them to order under abstract rules and purely technical procedures. Such rationality is embedded within the routines of everyday life as well as in the overarching structures of state, economy and society. It is understood to have marked our collective mentality so that it shapes our cultural outlook, intellectual orientations and psychological disposition. It determines the course of a substantial part of our lives.

I would not go so far as to suggest that the study of risk provides sufficient grounds from which to embark upon a full inquiry into the essential character of modern rationality and its multiple manifestations, but I do think that it is important to recognise that when it comes to studying either practices of risk assessment or analysing disputes over the contemporary meaning of risk, then at the same time we are inquiring into matters relating to the properties, value orientations and techniques of rationalisation. Where the language of risk features as a prominent component of social procedure and administrative process, we can frame this as an instance of institutional arrangements being set in place to rationalise human conduct. It is also the case that where controversies remain over the labelling of attitudes and behaviours as risk, then this can be approached either as an occasion where there is some ongoing dispute over the values dictating a particular course of rationalisation, or as an example of conflicts that flare up in response to movements to conform humanity to the rule of calculation and procedural control.

By studying risk we are presented with opportunities to magnify specific contexts of rationalisation so as to detail the social conditions, moral commitments, political movements, institutional arrangements and technical means by which these are made possible and are set upon their course. In other words, the concept of risk can be analysed as a cultural prism through which the character and tendencies of processes of rationalisation are brought into view. In the earlier period of the history of risk, these largely concern the development of techniques for promoting and consolidating the rationalisation of commercial life. By the middle of the nineteenth century, it is possible to trace movements to bring some of these techniques to bear upon social domains that up to that point remained beyond the technological and administrative reach of rationalisation, and here the social consequences and costs of these disciplinary measures become more open to political controversy and moral dispute. In recent times, the increasing conflicts of interpretation that have taken place with regard to the social value and meaning of various types of risk are associated with movements to conform people's health behaviours, occupational practices, leisure activities and patterns of consumption to measures of rational control which were largely unknown to previous generations. Where we can look back upon the semantic history of risk as one where increasing amounts of political controversy and social conflict have come to surround the ways this word features both as a referent of technical practice and as a category of everyday discourse, then at the same time, we are tracing paths towards a greater critical interrogation of the character and consequences of rationalisation.

In this regard, I hold to the view that Max Weber, the sociologist who above all others worked to uncover the origins and fate of modern rationality, can still teach us a great deal about risk. I also suggest that by casting debates on risk in Weberian perspective we can better appreciate the sociological value of his commitment to the analysis of rationalisation, and, further, the reasons behind the moral concerns he expressed over the impact of this process upon our lives.

A WEBERIAN CONCEPTION OF RISK

Most famously, in his essays on *The Protestant Ethic and the Spirit of Capitalism* (1958 [1904/5]), Weber sought to trace an 'elective affinity' between the rational organisation of modern capitalism and the 'worldly asceticism' of Puritan sects; however, it should not be forgotten that he also recognised the seeds of rational capitalism to have been sowed by developments within Western commerce that were not immediately connected to religion. In other writings, he investigates the contribution of changes in systems of law, administration and the organisation of labour relations within the promotion of rational conduct in economic affairs. In this regard, there are passages where he highlights the importance of rational bookkeeping for the early development of modern entrepreneurial capitalism (Weber 1978: 336–40). Weber is alert to the ways in which, at its origins, the economic life of Western European modernity was rooted in the commercial use of abstract calculations of probability that allowed for the future planning of capitalist enterprise on a scale without precedent. Whilst not dwelling in any detail on the concept of risk per se, he appears to recognise that advancements in techniques and practices of risk calculation were a vital component within the development of modern capitalism. Indeed, I would argue that at this point in his writing, he works to contextualise the practice of risk assessment as part of wider movements of rationalisation.

Beyond this, I hold that Weber's social theory has much more to bring to the analysis of risk; particularly when it comes to understanding the cultural dynamics of some of the disputes surrounding the contemporary use and meaning of this concept. Of most interest here are his writings on the problem of theodicy. Theodicy refers to the theological and/or philosophical attempt to justify the existence, character and justice of God (or gods) in face of a world that appears to contain an excessive amount of suffering. It is under the struggle to defend their religious convictions whilst confronted with the brute fact that suffering exists that many believers testify to experiencing the severest test of faith. For this reason, the problem of suffering might well be regarded as the bedrock of atheism, and there are passages where Weber suggests this is more likely than any other factor to lead to a loss of belief in the idea of God (Weber 1966: 139).

Weber is interested to trace the potential for people to adopt a secular outlook on life as the unintended consequence of efforts taken to uphold particular strands of theology (mostly associated with Protestantism) in face of the brute facts of human suffering. There are many aspects to his sociology of religion, but at various points he contends that it is at the point where religious cultures are made to explain 'the experience of the irrationality of the world' that we uncover a key dynamic within their propensity to change (Weber 1948a: 123, 1948b, 1948c). Indeed, beyond the bounds of explicitly religious worldviews, he holds that all human cultures are faced with the task of dealing with what appears to be an excessive amount of suffering in the world; in all times and places people struggle to find practical solutions to the pain of suffering and are compelled to work at making sense of this experience in terms of the overall meaning of their lives (Wilkinson 2005: 55–68). This component of human experience is a constant factor within wider processes of cultural and social change.

When confronted with a problem of suffering, Weber contends that in the first instance people tend to experience 'charismatic needs'; that is, an intense desire for some manner of release or escape from their affliction. This is often articulated in terms of religious longing, but may also be expressed through secular forms of utopian aspiration. Beyond this, he suggests that that while placed 'under the spur' of such needs, people tend to devote a great deal of energy to rationalising their situation (Tenbruck 1989: 70). Put simply, Weber argues that the problem of suffering drives people to find both the practical means to overcome their affliction and the ideal explanations that make sense of what they are experiencing in terms of their adopted way of life.

Frederich Tenbruck has famously argued that at this point we come across a distinctive premise in the cultural anthropology that underlies much of Weber's theorising on 'the social psychology of the world religions' (Tenbruck 1989; Weber 1948b). Weber claims that whilst struggling to come to terms with the problem of suffering people are often forced to change their practical behaviour as well as their intellectual outlook on life. The experience of suffering tends to change people's atti-tudes towards their existence, not only because of the ways in which it aggressively disrupts conditions of everyday life, but also through the unleashing of charismatic needs and the subsequent efforts that are taken to manage and control the excess of pain. People tend to be guided along particular courses of theoretical and practical solutions to their plight by the worldview they adhere to, and in the context of religious belief, Weber outlines the contours of the contrasting types of theodicy to be found in the major world religions. Each disposes people to adopt distinctive courses of action along with corresponding approaches to theorising their situation (Weber 1966: 138–49).

It is important to recognise here that Weber holds strongly to the view that all cultural outlooks on life are bound to fall short of providing peo-ple with a wholly sufficient means of dealing with 'the irrational force of life'. No matter when, where or how people live, they are always bound to come across painful experiences in life that they struggle to explain; peo-ple might have an elaborate set of reasons to rationally account for their experience, but these will never be sufficient to explain *all* they experi-ence. It is when placed under the burden to explain what appears to be an excessive amount of suffering in the world that reason is frequently tested to its limits and is all too often found wanting. In his studies of the world religions, Weber reflects upon the ways in which the struggle to accom-modate and/or vanquish 'the irrational force of life' serves to accentuate the logics at the heart of any worldview (Weber 1948c). He documents the ways in which believers are pressured to conform to an 'imperative of consistency'; that is, he is concerned to highlight a human compulsion to make the world conform to our cultural outlooks on life and/or modify those outlooks so that they are better adapted to explain lived experience (Weber 1948c: 324). Accordingly, Weber holds that, generally speaking, humans are psychologically disposed to organise the world around them so that it conforms to their ideal expectations, but at the same time, ideals may be moderated according to how they are sanctioned and/or disci-plined by the brute facts of experience. We struggle to live in existential discord, and when we encounter painful problems in life, these may well become unmanageable to a point where the desire to live in practical and intellectual harmony with the conditions of our existence becomes an all-consuming affair. Under this imperative of consistency we may even be moved to doubt our most cherished beliefs and radically change the ways we relate to the world.

Whilst analysing the dynamics of this complex within contrasting systems of religious belief, Weber works to highlight the distinctive components and human consequences of the culture of rationality that characterises our times. In this regard Talcott Parsons is alert to the radical implications of Weber's argument when he notes:

> Weber takes the fundamental position that, *regardless of the normative content of the normative order, a major element of discrepancy* [between normative expectations and actual experiences] is inevitable. And the more highly rationalized an order, the greater the tension, the greater the exposure of major elements of a population to experiences which are frustrating in the very specific sense, not merely that things happen that contravene their 'interests', but that things happen which are 'meaningless' in the sense that they ought not to happen. Here above all lies the problems of suffering and evil.
>
> (Parsons 1966: xlvii, emphasis original)

The process whereby a secular culture emerges as the unintended consequence of the cultural dynamics set within a particular form of Protestant theodicy is too lengthy and complicated to trace out here (Neiman 2002; Wilkinson 2005: 55–68). What is important to recognise is that whilst the idea of God may no longer hold much plausibility or be an immediate point of reference within modern people's accounts of how events take place in the world, the problem of suffering remains. Weber holds that the human compulsion to live under an imperative of consistency contributes its part to the eclipsing or death of God, but it never amounts to an adequate redress for the age-old problem of suffering. It might no longer be encountered in explicitly religious terms, but the problem of suffering always occupies a space in human experience; moreover, Weber appears to believe that, as a form of existential angst or moral dissonance, the problem of suffering is liable to be encountered as most problematic in societies that adhere to the most stringent courses of rationalisation. Put another way, the more that we expect our experience of life to 'add up' and conform to rational precepts, the more likely it is that we shall be morally scandalised by events that fail to match up to this expectation. There is a terrible sting in the tale here. Weber seems to be suggesting that the advance of modern processes of rationalisation comes at the cost of more intensive cultural encounters with 'the irrational force of life'.

At this point it might be useful to think with some examples. Everyday life in modern societies is conducted at almost every point through highly rationalised systems of management, efficiency and control. The design and manufacture of buses, trains, ferries and aeroplanes, the training of pilots, navigators and drivers, the timetabling of departures and arrivals, the implementation of health and safety checks and the handling of ticket sales are all instances of rationalisation. In all these activities, and in an inordinate amount of detail, social and natural environments are brought under the rule of calculation so that we can routinely travel around our countries and across the world. Under normal conditions we expect to depart on time and travel in safety to our chosen destinations and for every process en route to operate with efficiency. It is only on rare occasions that disaster strikes, but if a plane crashes, a train de-rails or a ferry sinks, there is sure to be a public outcry. Both as a matter of normative expectation and by the pattern of routine procedure such things most definitely should *not* happen. When rationalised systems fail in disaster, people not only experience and express a great deal of anger and upset, but are also deeply concerned to understand what went wrong and how measures can be set in place in order to prevent such events from taking place again. News media regularly report on disasters that occur because of the malfunctioning of modern technologies, the breakdown of expert systems of control or the malpractices and mistakes of professionals who normally can be relied upon to perform technical procedures with accuracy and efficiency. Following expressions of moral outrage, reports tend to move on to document details of official inquiries and legal proceedings that are designed to specify exactly what went wrong, who or what was to blame and recommend measures and interventions to ward off the possibility of further catastrophe.

When it comes to predicting and charting social responses to particular instances of catastrophe and human tragedy, we might anticipate that distinct cultures of moral argument, juridical process and political response will direct the specific courses of rationalisation that are pursued under the effort to restore order to the world. Each type of disaster can be associated with its own tradition of symbolic representation and established patterns of social disclosure and response. There are distinct elements to the cultural narratives and institutional behaviours that accompany the social upheaval and damage caused by fires, oil spills, hurricanes and floods that draw on the patterns of response set by similar events in the past. There may also be considerable variances in the ways in which social groups within and across nations attend to the causes and consequences of the calamities that befall them. Within the terms of the Weberian analysis that

I have outlined here, each event of disaster or instance of calamity can be studied in terms of its framing within a particular set of worldviews that serve both to amplify and to attenuate tendencies set within established processes of rationalisation. At the same time, one might anticipate that on every occasion where people encounter and/or experience excessive amounts of human suffering, then a common set of imperatives will be in evidence; namely, a desire to provide a satisfactory explanation for the event, a search for a right course of action to mitigate its deleterious effects on people's lives, and a concern for both ideal and practical solutions to comply to logics set by an overarching set of life principles. It is through tensions aggravated over the conflicts and inconsistencies experienced under the compulsion to fulfil these goals that the dynamics to wider processes of social and cultural change are set in motion.

I contend that the relevance of Weber for the sociological analysis of risk lies in the ways in which his work encourages us to approach debates over the social meaning and applications of this concept as instances where the value and course of rationalisation is held up for critical evaluation and moral scrutiny. In earlier sections of this chapter I charted the development of increasing levels of social dispute surrounding the meaning of risk. In the nineteenth century these disputes followed in the wake of moves by modern nation states to bring greater measures of control to bear upon the health, safety and welfare of populations. I argued that it was as a result of the heightened ambitions set for probabilistic thinking and the rational management of social problems that the clamour of debate surrounding matters of risk grew in range and volume. The level of moral and political debate that surrounds risk has increased along with the development of more sophisticated tools and elaborated projects of rationalisation.

It is possible to identify at least three arenas of risk debate in contemporary social science. The first concerns the ways in which modern science and industrial technologies are legitimated and used, particularly with regard to their negative impacts on the environment (Beck 1992; Loftedt and Frewer 1998; O'Mahony 1999). The second is focused on the legislative, administrative and technological means by which governments seek to manage welfare and social security (Culpitt 1999; O'Malley 2004; Taylor-Gooby 2000, 2004). The third charts the development of new institutional arrangements, social interventions and expert practices designed for the promotion of health and the ways in which different groups experience and respond to these (Heyman 1998; Petersen and

Wilkinson 2008). Each of these can be analysed as domains in which age-old problems of theodicy arise in a secular form. Risk debates almost invariably concern an experience or threat of suffering. Disputes surround the reality of possible dangers, the severity of experienced or potential harm, and extent to which a chosen course of action will serve to mitigate disaster. It might be more apt to refer to these as instances where matters of 'sociodicy' are raised; for what is being called into question here is the justice of social decision, the benevolence of social action and the moral rectitude of particular forms of social intervention.

I agree with Mary Douglas (see Chapter 3) that the fact that such disputes are conducted through a secular language of risk rather than with reference to theology bears testimony to the extent to which in our times, at least in relation to the issues listed above, most hold that it is more important to have the authority of technical experts and modern science than that of God and religious leaders on their side (Douglas 1992). However, whilst she draws on this insight to develop a Durkheimian analysis of social disputes about risk, here I am more concerned to highlight the ways this can be cast in Weberian terms. Weber depicts modern societies as fatefully immersed within processes of rationalisation that are bound on occasion to leave us morally scandalised when things go wrong. The more we are disposed to place an unquestioning faith in the efficiency of rational process and technical procedure the more likely it is that we shall be shocked and distressed when ideal expectations are betrayed by the harsh realities of lived experience. Beyond that, he offers us a means to analyse the forms of social psychology and action that tend to follow in the wake of a shattering of normative expectation. At this point, one of the more tragic elements of Weber's depiction of the rationality of our times lies in the suggestion that whilst constantly working to advance and improve systems and techniques of rationalisation (and often doing so in response to the threat or event of disaster), we are not only the heirs, but also the unwitting creators of cultural conditions that leave us poorly equipped to deal with occasions where the irrational force of life breaks into our existence. The problem of suffering is liable to be encountered with increasing intensity where everyday life is conducted under the expectation that nature and society will conform to the dictates of rationalisation.

Disputes about risk occupy the centre stage in societies where the terms of public debate are increasingly preoccupied with either the shortcomings and unintended consequences of particular forms of rationalisation or the social conflicts aroused by movements to exert heightened measures of procedural control over people's lives. Where attention is focused on actual or possible events of natural and/or technological disaster, we witness either breakdowns or unforeseen side-effects in modern processes of rationalisation (industrial technologies, systems of engineering, computer programming, health and safety procedures). On other occasions, where public disagreements surround the levels of risk courted through people's consumer habits, health behaviours and leisure activities, it is often the case that these revolve around attempts to introduce or increase the technical/expert regulation of everyday life; that is, we are witness to controversies fuelled by people's objections to the ways in which 'higher' authorities seek to regulate their bodies and behaviours. In addition to this, when it comes to movements for promoting the health and safety of our children, it may be more because of pressures 'from below' that processes of risk assessment and systems of rationalisation are made the objects of political and moral debate.

I have charted a path through the semantic history of risk whereby this concept has become increasingly open to conflicts of interpretation and is more frequently identified as a tool of ideology. I have argued that modern debates about risk are one of the ways in which the moral character and social purpose of processes of rationalisation are brought to the level of public debate. I contend that whilst Weber never imagined the extent to which matters of public health and environmental protection would come to political prominence in modern societies, he was certainly alert to the potential for any process of rationalisation to give rise to a host of social tensions and moral dilemmas when this was woven within the texture of everyday life. It is not only as a result of the ways in which the many episodes and discrete events in life confound the terms of normative expectation, but also with regard to the unforeseen and unintended consequences of many processes of rationalisation, that Weber understands us to have our attentions preoccupied by matters of theodicy; or as I have put it here, by questions of 'sociodicy'. Debates over the meaning and assessment of risk are just one instance of a cultural phenomenon that he held to be a constant factor within the dynamics of social change.

CONCLUSION

This chapter was written for the purpose of alerting readers to some of the domains of controversy surrounding the meaning of risk. One of my overriding aims here is to emphasise that, at least as far as the contemporary meaning of risk is concerned, we are always liable to be entering arenas of social conflict, moral anxiety and political dispute. There are always ideological interests at work where the language of risk is privileged as a means to label social problems, cultural attitudes and political objectives. The sociology of risk does not stand above the fray, but as sociology, it may be more inclined than other disciplines to work at understanding the cultural conditions and social means by which knowledge of the world is produced in these terms (Bourdieu 1993: 8–19).

By highlighting the value of a Weberian analysis of risk, I have worked to cast debates surrounding the meaning and use of this language within traditions of inquiry that reveal the cultural character, social conditions and human consequences of modern processes of rationalisation. I contend that this not only serves to bring sociological understanding to the history of risk, but also provides a vantage point from which to analyse the social interests and political motives that shape the ways this concept features in the everyday language of today's world. Hereby we might also be encouraged to re-read Weber and reappraise the relevance of his work for understanding the societies of our times. By no means do I consider Weber to provide us with the last word on risk. There is much more for us to consider here, but I hold strongly to the view that he still has an important contribution to make to any sociological assessment of this phenomenon.

By focusing so much attention on Weber, I have neglected some of the more conventional ways in which social theory is used to make sense of risk. This matter will be redressed in the chapter that follows. Here I have been concerned to open a door onto avenues of inquiry that have been largely forgotten or sidelined up to this point. In later chapters we shall return to Weber; for I hold that beyond the issues raised here, he still has more to bring to a critical appraisal of risk as well as the terms under which this now features as one of the 'unit ideas' of contemporary sociology.

3

RISK AND SOCIAL THEORY

A great deal of the sociological industry relating to the topic of risk is conducted in dialogue with developments in social theory that place this phenomenon at the centre of an attempt to unmask the distinctive cultural character of our times. Arguably it is the case that, along with matters relating to the intensification of processes of 'globalisation', 'individualisation' and 'reflexive modernisation', a concern to theorise social representations of risk and/or risk attitudes and behaviours is one of the central preoccupations of contemporary sociological theory. Indeed, some have moved to present social theories of risk as part of an attempt to re-fashion the language and concerns of sociological analysis so as to break with 'classical' frames of reference and reform the political directives and institutional goals of social science (Beck and Willms 2004; Gane and Beck 2004).

With reference to the discussion of the previous chapter, it is important to note that social theorists have become preoccupied with risk in a period where the conflict of interpretations over the social meaning of this concept is more pronounced than at any other time in history. Certainly, the contrasting and opposing ways in which theorists account for and evaluate risk bears testimony to this fact. In current social theory there is no agreement as to what the cultural prominence of matters of risk signifies for understanding the demands of our day; moreover, there is no consensus as to how risk should be defined and studied as a focal point of analysis. Accordingly, in so far as interests in risk have the potential to inspire new agendas of research, then from the outset we might anticipate that these shall be accompanied by a great deal of semantic and ethical dispute.

In this chapter, I provide a brief overview of the social theories that feature most prominently within the new sociology of risk. In each instance it is important to note that we are dealing with terms of debate that whilst offering a theoretical perspective on risk are also imbued with interests drawn from contrasting traditions of sociological inquiry. Social theorists are not so much interested in the topic of risk as they are with explaining institutional formations of society, dominant cultural trends and existing possibilities for large-scale social and political change. In contemporary social theory, a critical focus on risk takes place more out of a concern to analyse the social and cultural constitution of everyday life than with an interest in explaining people's relative aptitudes for probabilistic thinking or attitudes towards particular forms of hazard or danger.

In what follows, I make passing reference to some of the wider issues at stake within the sociological analysis of risk in the hope that this will suffice to encourage readers to engage in a broader project of study. I concentrate my attention on the favoured ways in which theorists make sense of risk and how this contributes to the overriding objectives of their work. My purpose is two-fold. First, I aim to underline the ways in which all social theorists share in the understanding that it is because of processes of social and cultural determination that individuals arrive at their relative points of view on matters of risk. In this regard, I highlight the (potentially) radical challenge that social theory brings to the field of risk analysis; namely, that all accounts of risk, including those of 'the actuarial expert', are shaped by institutional bias, social commitment and political preference. Indeed, this also involves me in bringing emphasis to the ways in which the institutional biases, moral commitments and political preferences of individual theorists contribute to their respective accounts of risk. Following on from this, the second aim is to sensitise readers to the ideological commitments at work within contrasting theoretical accounts of risk. Social theorists of risk are inclined to privilege modes of analysis in their work which at the same time incorporate a political commitment to a preferred vision of society and a selective emphasis upon particular dimensions of human agency. I hope to leave readers with a fuller appreciation for the extent to which the language of risk *always* comes ready laden with theoretical premises, ethical commitments and political interests. When adopting the concept of risk as a means to analyse organising principles of society or dominant modes of cultural consciousness and moral feeling we are unavoidably involving ourselves in ideologically stylised points of view on society.

The chapter begins with a critical comment on the ways in which social theory tends to feature within the expert domain of risk analysis. This is for the purpose of drawing some clear lines of distinction between the intellectual interests and institutional concerns that govern the actuarial account of risk as compared to those that feature within arenas of sociological theory. I argue that where experts in the field of risk analysis position social theorists along a linear dichotomy between 'realism' and 'social constructionism', this betrays a sociologically diminished account of risk and an account of social theory that is more disciplined to the interests of risk management than it is with advancing a critical questioning of the bearing of socio-cultural factors on individual attitudes and behaviours. I then move on to provide introductory and comparative outlines of the accounts of risk that are to be found in the works of Ulrich Beck, Mary Douglas and theorists of 'governmentality'. The overriding purpose of this chapter is to map out the conceptual terrain upon which debates about risk have come to occupy the attentions of contemporary social theory and inspire new avenues of inquiry for the sociological imagination. I am not so much interested in outlining the contribution of social theory to research in the field of risk analysis, but more with explaining the contribution of the analysis of risk to works of social theory.

BEYOND RISK ANALYSIS

In expert domains of risk analysis, the concept of 'risk' is taken to refer to a systematic process of probabilistic thinking that aims to identify the statistical likelihood that an adverse event will take place during a specified period of time. A classical expression of this positivistic notion of risk is found in a landmark Royal Society study group report in which the writers state that:

> [Risk is] the probability that a particular adverse event occurs during a stated period of time, or results from a particular challenge. As a probability in the sense of statistical theory risk obeys all the formal laws of combining probabilities.

> (The Royal Society 1992: 2)

On this account, by definition all risks are calculable and it is nonsense to suggest otherwise. Researchers have ratios, percentages and probabilities in mind when addressing their objects of study. Risk analysts employ sophisticated modelling techniques, mathematical theorems and methods of frequency analysis so as to arrive at a numerical expression of both the likelihood of a detrimental outcome resulting from a particular course of action and the magnitude of the adverse consequences that may follow on from this.

It is frequently observed that most people are not very good at estimating probabilities; whilst underestimating the potentially detrimental consequences of personal behaviours relating to smoking, the consumption of alcohol and sexual activity, most individuals tend to greatly overestimate the magnitude of risks to society associated with the activities of modern nuclear and chemical industries (Slovic 2000). The rule of thumb measures that are commonly used as a guide to conduct in everyday life are understood to obscure 'the reality of risk' so that people either underestimate the likelihood of bringing danger upon themselves or become excessively preoccupied with mitigating risks to society where the probability of experiencing some measure of harm appears remote in the extreme.

Whilst drawing on the findings of psychological research, most studies of lay perceptions of risk aim to 'scientifically' document the ways in which individuals *visualise*, *encode* and *mentally process* information relating to a select range of 'natural', 'social' and 'technological' hazards. Researchers then move on to debate the possible ways in which these might be shaped and modified so as to bring lay perspectives more in line with those of expert opinion. Experts in the field of 'risk communication' work at correcting 'inaccuracies' in the portrayal of scientific technologies in the public realm, and at the same time find ways of presenting 'the truth' about risks that are more in tune with people's intuitive capacities for processing such information. The overriding contention here is that it is possible to bolster the scientific rationality of popular understandings of the social costs and benefits of modern technologies, but this requires governments and scientists to concentrate their attentions upon improving the quality and production of public information about risk (Slovic 2000; Powell and Leiss 1997). However, at present few are prepared to place much confidence in existing practices of risk communication as the ideal means to achieve this goal. The hopes invested in public education campaigns as the immediate 'solution' to problems of risk perception are not matched by any good evidence to suggest that this is the most positive and reliable means to bring about the changes in individual's expressed thoughts and feelings about technological hazards that experts hope for (Fischoff et al. 1995; Jallinoja and Ayro 2000; Leiss 1996; Scholderer and Frewer 2003).

It is at this point that a door is opened onto the world of sociology. In the expert field of risk analysis, social theory tends to feature within efforts to explain why public opinion resists management and will not be persuaded to change; or rather, does not change in ways anticipated or desired by those working to manage lay understandings of risk. Whilst attributing a great deal of this to the 'stigmatised' ways in which matters of technological and scientific risk are portrayed in news media (Heimer 1988; Flynn et al. 2001; Pidgeon et al. 2003), some thoughts are given to the possibility that it may be as a result of a more elaborated process of social and cultural conditioning that people arrive at their favoured perspectives on risk. Accordingly, Paul Slovic, a leading figure in the field of risk perception research, concedes that insofar as individuals arrive at their opinions about the world whilst under the influence of wider social and political forces, then experts in the field of risk communication should be concerned not so much with simply educating the public as to the correct way to assess probabilities, but, rather, focus more of their attention on understanding the social conditioning of lay rationalities. At first, this insight leads him to caution that:

[R]isk debates are not merely about risk statistics, sociological and anthropological research implies that some of these debates may not even be about risk. ... Risk concerns may provide a rationale for actions taken on other grounds or they may be a surrogate for other social or ideological concerns. When this is the case, communication about risk is simply irrelevant to the discussion. Hidden agendas need to be brought to the surface.

(Slovic 1987: 285)

At this point, he does not appear to be prepared to admit to the extent to which such insight might also lead experts to reflect critically upon the social roles they perform and positions they occupy within society and the ways in which scientific endeavour, like all other social activities, comes under the influence of politics and ideology. However, in later works, whilst reflecting upon the limited achievements and frustrated ambitions of many technically prescribed solutions to public controversies surrounding industrial risk, he is moved to declare:

Scientific literacy and public education are important, but they are not central to risk controversies. The public is not irrational. ... The public is influenced by worldviews, ideologies and values. So are scientists, particularly when they are working at the limits of their experience. The limitations of risk science, the importance and difficulty of maintaining trust and the subjective and contextual nature of the 'risk game' point to the need for a new approach.

(Slovic 2000: 411)

Here Slovic underlines the fact that values are always at work in the ways in which 'adverse events' are categorised as such by expert assessors of risk, and, further, that the temporal frames that they consider relevant for calculating future probabilities are chosen from among many competing possibilities. He readily admits that cultural values and political preferences are embedded in the procedures by which statistical expressions of risk are formulated and presented for policy debate. Similarly, when it comes to weighing up the costs and benefits of risk, he acknowledges that scientific judgements are 'blended' with political decision, and, further, that the political conflicts that follow on from this point are more the result of a deficit in democratic process than the limitations of people's aptitudes for probabilistic thinking. Finally, in stressing the fact that risk research involves scientists working at *the limits of their experience*, he also raises a cautionary point that highlights a further value-laden feature of expert risk assessment; namely, that it incorporates the assumption that past experience (as categorised from a select point of view) is a reliable guide to the future. The technical assessment of risk is a technological quest to use knowledge of the past as a means to see beyond the limits of present experience so as to confront the future as knowable, predictable and law-like. This is a value commitment that involves scientists gambling with uncertainty and a number of commentators readily point to the fact that, despite the ever-increasing sophistication of instruments of quantitative data analysis, the future always retains a capacity to surprise us with discontinuities, irregularities and unanticipated extremes of behaviour that could not be adequately accounted for at the original point of risk assessment (Bernstein 1998). For the above reasons, Bob Heyman advises that we should never lose sight of the fact that a calculation of risk is a 'simplifying heuristic' which, for the sake of devising statements of probability, requires that we make many 'leaps of prognostication'. Calculations of risk provide us with glimpses of possible future realities, but at the same time, these possibilities are only made known through an imaginative exercise that requires us to think with cultural evaluations of past events, set frameworks of time and select perspectives on desirable outcomes that are always open to revision and conflicts of interpretation (Heyman 1998).

Sociology brings emphasis to the cultural relativity of risk perception. Sociological theories of risk offer contrasting accounts of the ways in which risk attitudes and behaviours are shaped according to our institutional affiliations and social commitments of everyday life. Experts in the analysis of risk may well draw upon this so as to present the 'social construction' of public opinion as a 'problem' for risk management, and there are many instances where social theory is employed as a means to cast people's social biases as politically suspect. There is no shortage of analysts who, whilst seemingly reluctant to debate with the political values that inform their preferred accounts of the reality of risk, are ready to use sociology as a means to expose the political choices and institutional preferences that inform competing visions of the possible futures that await us.

As I now move on to outline the core tenets of some of the most influential social theories of risk, readers should note that, whilst theorists present us with conflicting interpretations of the social meaning of risk, these are not formulated for the purpose of improving expert techniques of risk assessment. Social theorists are not disciplined to the interests of risk management. Indeed, in almost every instance, social theorists work to bring more emphasis to the analysis of power relations, political values and social ideology than to methods of quantification, modes of probabilistic thinking and individual capacities for probabilistic thinking. Beyond the expert domain of risk analysis, the sociological study of risk is largely preoccupied with debating the moral dynamics of our interpersonal and inter-institutional relationships; the direction of questioning is towards the kind of society we are in and the possibilities that exist for this to change.

RISK AS A PROBLEM FOR SOCIAL THEORY

In current social theory, the concept of risk features across a broad range of debates and by no means do these share in the same understanding of risk and its significance for social attitudes and behaviour. Theorists may well be concerned to investigate social perspectives on particular forms of danger so that the magnitude of perceived threats and the reality of dangers are raised as matters for debate, but sociological interests extend well beyond this point. In the domain of social theory, the concept of risk is also employed as a means to debate prevailing modes of self-identification and institutional affiliation and is studied on the understanding that it provides a critical vantage point from which to map out the dynamics of power relationships in contemporary society. Indeed, for some, the value of risk analysis lies not so much in the ways it serves as a means to investigate social responses to particular forms of possible danger, but more in the ways in which it might sensitise us to the ideological use of *language* in current policy debates surrounding individual responsibilities towards the state and how modern states are seeking to re-define notions of citizenship. There are three principle avenues of theoretical inquiry that comprise sociological approaches to risk. I shall outline each in turn so as to highlight key points of similarity and difference:

The 'risk society' approach

Ulrich Beck may be held largely responsible for bringing the concept of risk to prominence in contemporary social theory. The sociological industry on risk that followed in the wake of the publication of his book, *Risikogesellschaft: Auf dem Weg in eine Andere Moderne* (1986) which was later translated into English as *Risk Society: Towards a New Modernity* (1992), is a disciplinary defining event in recent social science. There are a number of possible explanations for this. In part, the popularity of Beck's work can be attributed to the fact that it occupied a vanguard position in sociological debates over the possible social impacts of the environmental crisis in an era of intensifying processes of globalisation. Moreover, at a time when many theorists were struggling to come to terms with the conviction that Marxism was no longer equipped to furnish the discipline with a framework suited to engage in a critical analysis of society, it is arguably the case that Beck's work was read in the hope that it offered a means to reinvigorate radical traditions of sociological inquiry. Certainly, he has been prepared to defend his work on these terms, and at the same time as Anthony Giddens sought to redefine his sociological project as an analysis of 'the consequences of modernity' with a view to advancing a new programme for social democracy, Beck's publications were referenced on the understanding that they charted the emergence of new forms of political consciousness and motivation (Beck 1994, 1997; Hutton and Giddens 2000; Giddens 1990, 1991, 1994).

There is now a considerable conflict of interpretations surrounding Beck's work (Gabe 2004). In part this may be because of a lack of care on his part when it comes to documenting the expository roles and critical purposes of key terms of analysis, but beyond this, the volume of his output, his apparent willingness to adapt his thesis so as to engage with a wide variety of audiences and the fact that he often appears to approach the task of writing more with a mind to provoke debate than with the aim of outlining a systematic approach to thinking means that it is now possible to chart a number of interpretive paths through his work. One should not expect to find any consensus when it comes to determining the right balance of emphasis between his principle claims and concerns.

Beck's concerns for the topic of risk have always revolved around an interest in the potential for the experience and/or threat of catastrophe to shock people into a radical questioning of received wisdom and established convention. In the technical domain of risk analysis, the concept of risk refers to a calculation of probability, however, in Beck's account, the concept is used to draw attention to 'incalculable' domains of threatening uncertainty. There is a strong political thrust to his writing and in recent works this has featured to a point where he readily declares that above all else his interests concern the ways in which perceptions of risk have the 'political power' to 'explode self-referential systems and national and international political agendas, overturning their priorities and producing practical interconnections among mutually indifferent or hostile parties and camps' (Beck 2006: 36). For Beck, 'risk' is a synonym for large-scale hazards that are peculiar to recent social and technological developments within conditions of modernity; moreover, his concern for the analysis of such phenomena is focused above all else upon the project of how modern societies might be made to embark upon a course of radical social change.

Beck maintains that Western modernity stands on the brink of global 'self-annihilation'. He argues that we are 'caught in the trap that the world has become' (Beck 1995a: 98–106). A new 'era of disasters' is upon us; disasters which prevailing conditions of industrial modernity have brought upon themselves. On this account, a world revolution will soon be upon us, but a revolution quite unlike any other in modern history. This revolution will be system self-induced; it will arise from conditions produced 'automatically' and 'unreflectingly' and will gather to a storm 'on the basis of modernity's blindness to apocalypse' (ibid.). For Beck, the most important questions confronting sociology concern the possibility of managing the crisis in which we find ourselves and transforming the ways in which we live so as to create social conditions in which processes of modernisation can take place with due regard for global ecology and world democracy.

Beck first announced his thesis on the 'risk society' in the aftermath of disasters such as the Union Carbide chemical plant disaster at Bhopal on 3 December 1984 and the Chernobyl nuclear plant disaster of 26 April 1986 and consequently highlighted the prospect of future nuclear and chemical contaminations as the most alarming threats to modern civilisation. The list has now lengthened to include AIDS, livestock diseases such as foot and mouth disease and avian flu, scientific controversies surrounding genetic technologies (particularly in relation to the manufacture of foods), the uncontrollability of global markets and the threat of terrorist attacks (Beck 2002, 2005: 243–4, 2006: 33–4). On this account, the characteristics that unite such hazards are: first, that they exist as unintended 'side-effects' of processes of technological and scientific modernisation; second, that there is so much uncertainty surrounding the potential magnitude of the disasters that they may visit upon society that may be categorised as *incalculable* risks; third, that they cannot be contained within national borders and have a potential to wreak havoc on a global scale, and finally, that they each *confront* modern societies with *demands* for mitigation and restitutive action for the sake of planetary survival.

Beck's representation of the reality of the risks we face is open to a great deal of critical debate and he readily admits to this. In some of the more cautious passages of his writing, he notes that 'hazards are subject to historico-cultural perceptions and assessments which vary from country to country, from group to group, from one period to another' (Beck 1995a: 91), and that the rationality of risk perception is always open to social definition (Beck 1992: 59). Indeed, because of the extent to which many of these risks are not made immediately available to sensory experience and only become 'socially available' to us via media pictures and reports, he is sometimes moved to portray the 'risk society' as a kind of 'shadow kingdom' where the potential for global catastrophe remains a matter for speculation (Beck 1995a: 100), but, nevertheless, more often than not he works with an emphasis upon the conviction that we are living only a hair's breadth away from a terminal period of global disaster.

The prospect of global calamity forms the back-drop to much of his theorising on the fate of modernity; indeed, it is a most vital component of his account of the forms of emancipatory politics with which we might live towards the future. Beck does not regard the advent of risk society as the grounds for pessimism or as a reason to indulge in 'postmodern panic' (Bailey 1988; Barrett 2001; Kroker and Cooke 1988); rather, he draws hope from the possibility that these might be the only conditions under which societies can be moved towards 'ecological enlightenment' (Beck 1995b). He argues:

> This all-encompassing and all-permeating insecurity is not just the dark side of freedom. What is important is to discover it as the bright side. The intro-duction of insecurity into our thoughts and deeds may help to achieve the reduction of objectives, slowness, revisability and ability to learn, the care, consideration, tolerance and irony that are necessary for the change to a new modernity.
>
> (Beck 1997: 168)

From his point of view, the greater our collective imagination for disaster, the more likely it is that we shall be moved to engage with the 'reinvention' of politics (Beck 1997, 1999). For Beck, 'risk consciousness' is a necessary part of the means by which populations are primed to engage in public debates over the possible futures which await us and the types of social conditions in which humanity might survive and prosper. Moreover, he argues that insofar as modern individuals are increasingly made to nego-tiate with uncertainties in work and family relations, then the day-to-day insecurities experienced as personal risks also predispose us to become anxiously preoccupied with large-scale risks to society as a whole. Whilst the 'risk society' thesis aims to divulge the political meaning of particular types of global hazard, it also offers a perspective on the ways in which the public information about the portents of disaster is likely to be received among populations experiencing accelerated processes of 'individualisa-tion' arising from the flexibilisation of the labour process and transfor-mations in popular attitudes towards love and family life (Beck 1992, 2000b; Beck and Beck-Gernsheim 1995, 2002). Beck represents the com-mon experience of a 'risk society' as one where the majority of individu-als are fraught with anxieties of self-identity and social purpose, and as they gather every evening around 'the village green of television', he claims that more than ever before they are bound to become consciously aware of the fact that problems of global society are entwined with their personal biographies and fate (Beck 1992: 131–8).

Beck's hope is that such conditions serve to nurture the *cosmopolitanisation* of our political outlooks, institutional practices and personal behaviours; indeed, in more recent works he maintains that this process is already well rooted and established as a vital element within new forms of *global* civil society and polity. He declares:

Cosmopolitanisation ... [is] a multidimensional process that has irrevocably changed the historical 'nature' of social worlds and the status of individual countries within those worlds. It involves the formation of multiple loyalties, the spread of transnational lifestyles, the rise of non-state political actors (from Amnesty International to the World Trade Organisation), and the development of global protest movements against (neo-liberal) globalism and for a different (cosmopolitan) globalisation involving worldwide recognition of human rights, worker's rights, global protection of the environment, an end to poverty and so on. All these tendencies may be seen as the beginning, however deformed, of an institutionalised cosmopolitanism – paradoxically in the shape of anti-globalisation movements, an International Criminal Court or the United Nations.

(Beck 2004: 136)

In the final analysis, Beck's interest in the topic of risk is shaped above all else by the conviction that modern individuals, capitalist markets and national states *must* change their outlooks and behaviours and engage in a project of planetary survival for the common good of humanity across the globe. By focusing on risks as 'large-scale hazards' that represent the threat of global annihilation, he aims to underline the urgent requirement for a wholesale political reformation of the institutional logics that govern capitalist economies and the modern nation state. He looks to an increasingly powerful transnational community of non(or quasi)-governmental organisations to bring an end to the reign of party politics focused on national-state directed agendas; he holds to the view that as populations are made 'world-risk conscious', the motive force of anxiety directed towards the task of saving ourselves from extinction will serve as a major spur towards the achievement of this goal.

Beck's sociological ambition is overtly political and his mode of analysis is polemically geared to promote a strident account of a society living on the brink of global catastrophe. His diagnosis is alarming and his prescription calls for no less than a project of radical social change on a global scale. Here, the sociological investment in the topic of risk is far removed from any technical debate over formal aspects of risk assessment or individual aptitudes for probabilistic thinking. Beck only has eyes for the possibility of radically transforming the way we live now. He is adamant that current processes of modernisation are set on a course of environmental and social destruction that ultimately leads to the annihilation of life on earth. It is only in so far as populations are made conscious of the fact that they are living in a 'world risk society' that they shall come to understand that their best hopes for survival lie in the direction of a new age of 'cosmopolitan' democracy, and his later works are devoted to disclosing the social conditions under which this might yet be brought into reality.

Mary Douglas and cultural theory

A second major influence over sociological theories of risk is the 'cultural theory' devised by Mary Douglas. Here we are presented with an account of risk which is very different to that found in the works of Ulrich Beck; indeed, whilst she does not appear to seek a direct confrontation with Beck, a great deal of her work can be read as designed to cast suspicion upon the visions of social reality upheld by radical critics of society. Certainly, in so far as sociological theories of risk provide a context for debating the magnitude and social effects of a global environmental crisis, Douglas moves to promote a form of politics that stands opposed to the 'alarmism' that characterises the approach of non-governmental organisations such as Greenpeace and Friends of the Earth.

Mary Douglas presents her research in terms of a project to elaborate upon the later works of Emile Durkheim relating to the ways in which modes of community and social organisation determine the cultural categories through which people express their social feelings and offer explanations for events in the world (Durkheim 2001; Durkheim and Mauss 1963; Douglas 1978a). On this account, the ways in which individuals articulate and explain the meaning of their lives is always shaped by the quality of their prior commitments to social groups and communities of belonging. A group mentality always stamps its mark upon the personality and psychology of its members, and it is this which directs people's convictions when they are moved to voice their most cherished beliefs about the character of society and how they should live as good citizens.

Douglas argues that throughout human history, when the binds of social solidarity are weakened, it is commonplace for people to become preoccupied with the threat of disaster. When people lose their sense of belonging, they react by evoking shared beliefs about impending catastrophe, and this has a *positive* function for society. She maintains that in so far as people's minds are preoccupied with images of impending disaster, then not only it is likely that they shall be motivated to quash movements towards group disunity, but they shall also stand united around a common set of social objectives; that is, they shall be morally energised to work together in order to protect their group from harm. In addition to this, a common strategy for group survival involves a search for 'others' to blame and Douglas regards such behaviour as both contributing to the creation of a stronger sense of group identity (i.e. 'we' are not like 'others') and as providing a shared outlet for expressions of anxieties built up whilst sensing possible danger. Here it is important to note that she holds that the intensity of people's sense of alarm in face of future hazards is not determined so much by the character and magnitude of a perceived danger, but, rather, is conditioned by the quality of the social ties that bind them to their group.

Whilst Ulrich Beck works to emphasise the novelty of the 'mega-hazards' of industrialisation and appears convinced that we are confronted with social circumstances and institutional formations for which there is no historical precedent, by contrast, Mary Douglas is inclined to stress the cultural relativity of hazard perception and regards collective representations of apocalypse as a common form of social response when communal bonds are strained. She argues that the collective imagination for disaster functions throughout history as a source of moral legitimation for community and as a cultural instrument for the maintenance of group solidarity. Douglas moves to contextualise current public concerns about a society 'at risk' within a tradition of sociological understanding that aims to expose the ways in which people's deeply held cultural beliefs about their origins and fate perform an integrative function in the maintenance of group solidarities. She contends that contemporary debates about risk are essentially akin to age-old religious discourses of theodicy (Douglas 1992: 26). Where people once spoke of being 'sinned against', they now talk about being 'at risk'. Douglas argues that in cultures placed under the influence of modern process of secularisation, the language of 'risk' has taken the place of the language of 'sin'. Both are languages of blame. The concept of risk is the modern device for calling those who have 'sinned against' us to repent for their wrongdoing so as to bring justice and restore order to the world. The main difference is that where the language of sin appeals to the authority of priests and divine law, the language of risk appeals to the authority of science and the prophetic powers of modern rationality.

With regard to current preoccupations with impending environmental catastrophe, she maintains that the fear of ecological apocalypse has come to occupy a cultural position which is much the same as belief in 'The Day of Judgement'. Indeed, she moves to suggest that in secular consciousness, 'Nature' has replaced 'God' as the moral judge of society. Where in religious cultures individuals evoke the wrath of God so as to voice their complaint towards 'others' that are perceived to pose a threat to their group, in secular societies this takes place through the portent of global environmental disaster. As far as Douglas is concerned, 'either the backlash of God, or the backlash of nature is an effective instrument for justifying group membership' and when framed as a major 'risk' to society, the threat of environmental disaster can be readily used as 'a stick to beat authority' (Douglas 1990: 4; Douglas and Wildavsky 1982: 127).

Mary Douglas's 'cultural theory' offers a sociological explanation for conflicts of opinion over the reality and magnitude of the risks we face. Her 'grid-group' system of social classification has been adopted by a number of theorists with interests in offering their services to industries and governments concerned with the 'management' of public opinion in relation to 'official' methods of 'risk communication' (Dake 1992; Douglas 1978b; Ellis 1993; Rayner 1992; Schwarz and Thompson 1990; Thompson et al. 1990; Wildavsky and Dake 1990). Within this framework of analysis, all members of society are considered to belong to one of four distinct cultural groupings. Depending upon the extent to which individuals are integrated within bonds of community and according to quality of the moral commitments they hold towards values upheld by state authorities, they are classified as hierarchists, individualists, egalitarians and fatalists.

It is argued that each group has its own distinctive cultural outlook on reality that is shaped by the quality of individual's social commitments to a preferred 'way of life', and that this is particularly in evidence when it comes to each group's favoured political outlook and their depictions of 'nature' and 'society'. Individualists are understood to support social institutions that place a particular value on the goal of personal freedom and tend to regard nature as robust and amenable to technological change. Individualists are liberal in their political outlook and are inclined towards entrepreneurship in relation to their occupational behaviour. Hierarchists are represented as committed to a lifestyle which regards time-honoured tradition and establishment values as the bedrock of good society. Hierarchists are conservative in their political outlook and are readily prepared to allow past custom to set the standard for judging what is environmentally acceptable when it comes to technological interventions in nature. Egalitarians are portrayed as committed to ideals of redistributive justice and as being inclined to their support to institutions that challenge the hierarchical structure of society on behalf of the common good. Their political values are geared to support initiatives taken on behalf of institutionally disadvantaged sectors of society and this tends to incorporate a 'green' attitude towards nature. It is egalitarians who are most inclined to campaign on behalf of maintaining environmental health and safety. Finally, fatalists are identified as socially isolated individuals who do not have any strong group affiliations. They have no strong views when it comes to politics or nature; rather, their cultural outlook is characterised by a predisposition to rationalise their perceived inability to exercise any significant measure of influence over events in the world.

Douglas understands the increasing amounts of public debate surrounding the environmental crisis as a sign that egalitarianism is on the increase in Western societies. She maintains that this development is in large part related to a wider crisis of social solidarity. In particular, she holds that the intensifying force of 'globalisation' upon the world capitalist economy is liable to leave individuals feeling more vulnerable under conditions of day-to-day life, and this has the further consequence of agitating worries about threats to the environment. On this account, in a move similar to Beck's position on the social impacts of individualisation, she holds that people's anxieties over conditions of work and family life feed into their expressed concerns over wider risks to society.

However, Douglas's analysis stands in marked contrast to that of Beck when it comes her regard for popular concerns relating risks to the environment, for she considers the cultural resonance of such matters as more of an expression of Durkheimian anomie than an appropriate response to the reality of danger. She advises that we should understand the apocalyptic concerns of environmental pressure groups as a surrogate means by which egalitarian groups deal with their problems of social solidarity. Douglas holds that the shared sense of alarm in face of the threat of environmental disaster functions both to strengthen the unity of egalitarian social groups and to provide a means of identifying 'others' to blame for threats brought to their way of life.

Such a perspective draws heavily upon the understanding that when it comes to predicting the future, no one can claim to know precisely what this holds, and, further, that conflicts of interpretation and competing judgements will always surround the reality and magnitude of the risks facing humanity. When faced with disagreements over these matters, Douglas maintains that we arrive at our preferred points of view on possible futures more as a result of placing our *trust* in favoured sources of information than as a response to an 'objective' analysis of the facts at hand. Quite simply, in this context, it is impossible to arrive at an 'objective' point of view on the world. Too much controversy surrounds the truth status of the 'facts' of matter, and we have no choice but to choose our preferred scenario on the grounds of trust. Accordingly, favoured renditions of the reality of risk are more an expression of faith in a particular group's cultural outlook on life than a proportional response to real danger.

Within cultural theory, most critical analysis is directed towards the egalitarian outlook and way of life; for a key contention here is that their inclination to support radical environmental agendas is likely to be fuelled more as a response to problems of group solidarity than by a measured account of the reality of risks we face. Following Douglas most cultural theorists are inclined to regard the hierarchist outlook as most trustworthy. They tend to regard state authorities and government experts as best placed to assess the reality of risk on behalf of the common good, for they contend that when it comes to deciding whose version of social reality is most credible, we should side with those who are charged with the task of dealing with the adverse consequences of real events of disaster. In the final analysis, Douglas advises that we make a pragmatic decision, which is to entrust ourselves to those who are best organised to defend society when disaster strikes (Douglas and Wildavsky 1982). Accordingly, whilst Beck is inclined to lend his support to environmental pressure groups campaigning outside and against the state, Douglas is more of a mind to entrust herself to the state's providence and safe-keeping. Once again, a political message is to the fore within the analysis of risk, albeit one which stands opposed in many respects to that advanced by Beck.

Governmentality and risk

Arguably, it is in the hands of theorists of 'governmentality' that the greatest efforts are made to bring questions of power and politics to the fore within the analysis of risk. Working under the influence of Michel Foucault, writers such as Robert Castel, Ian Culpitt, Mitchell Dean, François Ewald and Pat O'Malley urge us to be particularly attentive to the ways in which the language of risk features within social policy as a means to co-ordinate society as a nexus 'power relations' (Castel 1991; Culpitt 1999; Dean 1999a; Ewald 1986; O'Malley 2004). They hold to the view that in the current widespread use of the language of risk in political and administrative/regulatory discourse, we are presented with opportunities to elaborate upon Foucault's analysis of 'the rationality of government' (Burchell et al. 1991).

Whilst centring their analysis of risk on the theme of 'governmentality', these researchers are more directly inspired by Foucault's commentaries on the interrelationship between power and subjectivity. In his essay on 'governmentality', Foucault is principally concerned to sketch out a research project that traces the origins and development of governmental apparatuses for the exercise of power over and within the administrative structures and populations of Western nation states (Foucault 1991). Certainly, government legislation that incorporates a language of risk might be studied as representing a new chapter within this history; however, when it comes to interpreting the social meaning of risk, theorists of 'governmentality' tend to draw more upon the ideas outlined in Foucault's 'Afterward' in 'The subject and power' that is included at the end of an edited collection of essays by Hubert Dreyfus and Paul Rabinow (Foucault 1982). It is in an earlier French version of this paper that Foucault provides the phrase that is often cited as a means to summarise the interest of theorists of governmentality in relation to risk; namely, 'the conduct of conduct' ('l'exercice du pouvoir consiste à *conduire des conduites* et à aménager la probabilité) (Foucault 1984: 314).

Foucault claimed that he was principally concerned to provide a history of the institutional settings and procedures in which 'human beings are made subjects', but in this he acknowledged that the analysis of power relations came to occupy an increasingly important position in his work (Foucault 1982: 208–9). When Foucault writes about *power* he does not have in mind the domination of one group over another, but, rather, an elaborate exercise between partners where one leads the other in their conduct, but only to the point where the one being led may act within a broad 'field of possibilities'. With the term 'power relations', Foucault seeks to refer us to the ways in which individuals and groups are directed to take up behaviours which at the same time they choose to adopt as their preferred way of living; power relations are an integral component of an exercise in 'government' which aims 'to structure the possibilities of action of other people' (Foucault 1982: 220–1).

The main claim advanced by contemporary theorists of governmentality is that, in recent years, the language of risk has been widely adopted as a primary technique of government (in the Foucauldian sense of the word). On this account, when attitudes and behaviours are officially labelled as 'risk', then efforts are being made to conduct people so that they in turn *conduct themselves* along a select course of action and towards a particular set of goals. There are many contexts where the language of risk now features as a principle means to achieve 'the conduct of conduct'. Perhaps most notably, it appears in health promotion campaigns where the intention is to advise people that if they are to minimise the risk of contracting heart disease, then they should exercise regularly and avoid eating certain foods. Similarly, whenever the language of risk is used as part of an authoritative warning that it is in our best interests to pay for insurance against personal damage and loss, save for the future with the latest pension scheme, fit our homes with security systems and carry out precautionary behaviours to guard ourselves against physical assault, then an exercise in power relations is identified as taking place whereby individuals are being directed (for the sake of their own interests) to guard themselves from harm. Indeed, Mitchell Dean works harder than most to emphasise the distinguishing characteristics of the account of risk that takes places under the auspices of 'governmentality' when he writes:

> There is no such thing as risk in reality. Risk is a way – or rather, a set of different ways – of ordering reality, of rendering it into a calculable form ... the significance of risk does not lie in risk *itself* (original emphasis) but with what risk gets attached to ... risk [should be] analysed as a component of assemblages of practices, techniques and rationalities concerned with how we govern. ... In the 'governmental' account, risk is a calculative rationality that is tethered to assorted techniques of regulation, management, and shaping of human conduct in the service of specific ends and with definite, but to some extent unforeseen, effects.
>
> (Dean 1999b: 131–2)

From this perspective, the sociological importance of risk does not lie so much in the ways in which the concept is used to draw public attention to particular types of danger or as a device for the maintenance of group solidarities; rather, an emphasis is placed upon the ways in which, at this particular juncture in our cultural history, the language of risk features as part of a governmental framework which is creating new forms of subjectivity and redefining the moral outlooks that we bring to our interpersonal relationships and political expectations. Most importantly, whilst both Beck and Douglas are inclined to explain the public prominence and cultural preoccupation with risk as, in part, a response to social processes of individualisation, theorists of 'governmentality' identify the language of risk as actively involved in promoting this process. The new forms of subjectivity and types of social relationship that are co-ordinated through risk-based government are understood to be geared towards promoting an ethic of 'individual responsibility' and 'freedom of choice' across society.

Most theorists of governmentality are highly critical when it comes to evaluating the sociological consequences of this development, for they hold that the 'freedom of choice' advanced within this governmental strategy is redolent with the interests of neo-liberal capitalism. A great deal of research into 'governmentality' is explicitly geared towards highlighting the ideological processes by which governments in Britain and Australia are seeking to introduce market principles within the management of health, education and social security (Petersen 1996; Dean 1999b). Here it is argued that where principles of 'risk management' and 'risk communication' are brought to bear within the policy and practice of welfare provision, then the overriding purpose (which is seldom made explicit for public debate) is to transfer responsibility for precaution and prevention from the state to the individual. Accordingly, the introduction of a language of risk within current government legislation and social policy is understood to betray a commitment to a 'New Right' political agenda that stands fundamentally opposed to the social democratic ethos of universal welfare provision and state intervention on behalf of the collective good (Kemshall 2002).

According to Nikolas Rose, this shift in the ethos of government may hold even more drastic consequences for sociological thinking. He argues that the growth of industries of 'risk management' and 'risk communication' contributes to 'the death of the social' as a category of self-understanding and as an object of political interest (Rose 1996). Rose maintains that as social problems and social behaviours are labelled as 'risks' and where individuals are categorised as 'at risk', then more often than not a governmental strategy is at work that aims to conduct individuals towards the view that they should '*take upon themselves* the responsibility for their own security and that of their families' (Rose 1996: 341–2). From a sociological point of view the great danger here is that where social problems, social attitudes and social behaviours are addressed in terms of 'portfolios of risk' or as matters of 'risk perception', then the *social* component of these factors is eclipsed in favour of factors pertaining to the individual. He is alarmed by the possibility that the 'risk society' promotes a limited account of society as comprised by an aggregate of disparate individuals all sharing in a common cultural experience and fate; a society that pays no heed to the bearing of socio-economic class divisions upon the experience of health, education and social opportunity. Rose contends that in public risk discourse, the most vital questions concerning existing possibilities for social change tend to be divorced from debates over political economy, and, rather, are addressed solely as matters for personal education and moral reform at the level of 'the individual' (Rose 1990, 1999).

Yet again, within the perspective of 'governmentality', the sociological account of risk is geared to promote a particular approach to thinking about the dominant characteristics of society and its propensity to change. In contrast to Beck and Douglas, the attempt to understand the ways in which individuals and groups perceive the reality of particular types of danger is not a major focus of concern; it is not the realities referred to by the concept of risk, but, rather, the moral texture of this kind of language which is of most interest. Whilst within the bounds of 'cultural theory' and accounts of 'world risk society', people are understood to become increasingly preoccupied with risk as part of a response to social pressures towards individualisation, according to theorists of governmentality we should rather understand the language of risk as an integral component of this process. It is not so much that individualisation gives rise to risk consciousness, but rather that conceptualising the social world in terms of risk promotes an individualising worldview. Once again, political questions are brought to the fore within the sociological analysis of risk, but here these may well be turned back upon the most elemental component sociological thinking; namely, the category of 'the social' itself. Where for Beck and Douglas the analysis of risk serves as a means to advance modes of sociological thinking that bring questions of society to the fore, from the perspective of writers such as Nikolas Rose, the sociological adoption of risk as a primary unit of analysis might well serve to stunt the development of proper sociological thinking.

CONCLUSION: THE SOCIOLOGICAL DOMAIN
OF RISK ANALYSIS

In a number of recent introductions to the topic of risk, sociological interests are framed via an analysis of 'realist' and 'social constructionist'
accounts of the world (Adams 1995; Lupton 1999; Denney 2005).
Accordingly, the difference between contrasting sociological approaches
to the study of risk lies in the extent to which researchers bring emphasis
to the relative ways in which knowledge about risk is determined by cultural values and forms of social belonging. Whilst making reference to an
'objective' actuarial account of risk, sociology is often introduced into the
discussion as a means to debate the bearing of 'subjective' and contingent
factors in people's everyday beliefs about the reality, quantity and scale of
risks they face. By contrast, I contend that by positioning social theorists
of risk along a linear dichotomy between 'realism' and 'social constructionist' one is left with both a diminished understanding of risk as well as
a restricted account of sociology. I hold to the view that 'objectivity' is a
social value and what we accept as 'objective' knowledge about our world
is always shaped by the quality of our social commitments and cultural
worldviews. With regard to debates about risk, we are always dealing with
factors of uncertainty where no unanimous agreement can be found on
the possible futures that await us. Under these circumstances individuals
are always bound to defer to convictions based on social trust and cultural
disposition. The value of sociology lies in its capacity to expose the ways
in which public debates over the reality and magnitude of risks are related
to the social distribution and exercise of power; that is, sociological
research is particularly well suited to bring emphasis to the ideological
interests at work within the cultural production and social representation
of knowledge about risk. On this account, no one is in a position to lay
claim to a politically neutral, value-free, or incontrovertibly objective
account of risk; rather, risk always gives voice to positions of social bias,
cultural commitment and political preference.

   In domains of expert analysis the concept of risk is used to refer to a
calculation of probability, but in popular usage it is more likely to appear
as a synonym for danger. Social theorists present us with a range of interpretive frameworks for debating what is morally and politically at stake
when 'risk' is used in the language of everyday life, particularly when this
is brought to the fore as the signature motif of news reports on the problems of our day. Social theory presents the concept of risk as replete with

ideological meaning. For social theory, the study of risk does not so much require that we investigate people's aptitudes for probabilistic thinking as expose the social interests at work and the exercise of power invested in the ways the language of risk is used to highlight social problems, attitudes and behaviours as cause for alarm. On this understanding, if we leave the ideological purpose of the language of risk outside of our sphere of analysis, then we are closing the door on a proper sociological understanding of the meaning of risk in society.

In this chapter I have also highlighted the potential for the ideological bearings of risk to exert an influence over the politics of social theory; or rather, I have underlined the ways in which the language and analysis of risk is appropriated by social theorists as a means to cast their accounts of society in political and moral perspective. In the previous chapter I stressed that when it comes to charting a path through the many debates and controversies that surround the contemporary meaning of risk that sociology does not (and cannot) stand above the fray. This is certainly the case when the concept of risk is privileged as a means to theorise society. I contend that our sociological maturity lies in honing the ability to understand and make clear the values on which the foundations of theories are set and the political purposes for which they are put to use.

4

RISK IN SOCIAL CONTEXT

There is more to sociology than questions of power and politics. Whilst social theorists of risk are chiefly preoccupied with the ideological bearing of risk discourse upon society, it is possible to find many other forms of sociological inquiry into this phenomenon. In this respect, there is the important matter of establishing the social meaning of risk in everyday life. A great deal of sociological work is not so much concerned with advancing frameworks for the analysis of politics and power relations, but, rather, is committed to exposing the ordinary and situated ways in which individuals and groups perceive, talk about and respond to risk across a broad range of institutional contexts and social settings.

To some readers it may seem strange to note that in many instances there is a lack of fit between the theoretical discourse of sociology and discoveries made through empirical research. Certainly, in the context of risk research, findings drawn from empirical studies of risk attitudes and behaviours often serve to cast suspicion on claims advanced at the level of theory. Arguably, it is the case that when brought under the demand for empirical research evidence, substantial components of proposals raised by cultural narratives on 'risk and modernity' are exposed as no more than castles in the air; they appear too far removed from the social realities of everyday life (Irwin et al. 1999; Wilkinson 2001b). More often than not, when priority is given to interpreting the wider cultural and/or political meanings of risk in our times, then commentators pay little heed to the task of establishing how people actually talk about and respond to this (if at all!) as a matter of everyday social routine; the high tones of 'academic' discourse are favoured to the cost of opinions expressed in the 'ordinary' languages of work and family life. All too easily it seems that when sights are set upon advancing a 'grand theory' of society, the empirical task of detailing the ways in which problems of risk feature in lived experience is treated as a peripheral concern.

In this chapter I provide a critical overview of empirical research into risk attitudes and behaviours. This serves to highlight some of the discrepancies between the representations of risk society found in social theory and discoveries made though empirical research. However, it also draws attention to the methodological problems faced by researchers venturing into the field. Indeed, rather than amend theoretical conceptions of risk society with empirical understanding, I suggest that, in many instances, empirical studies of risk attitudes and behaviours have done more to highlight problems of research design and practice. In the final analysis, I hold that these methodological problems are of such an order that the cumulative findings of empirical studies of risk perception research serve more to underline our ignorance about the lived experience of risk than make this clear to sociological understanding.

A key point of contention here concerns the analytical status of 'social context' and the ways this is made the object of research. I hold that it is vitally important to appreciate the bearing of social context upon the ways in which individuals perceive and respond to risk. It is only by attending to social context that it becomes possible to piece together an understanding of how, under 'normal' circumstances, individuals are most likely to interpret and respond to knowledge about risk. I argue that the importance of this matter is such that it should be recognised as the pivotal factor of analysis within studies of the social meaning of risk in everyday life.

Insofar as most studies of risk perception tend to concentrate upon the ways individuals think about risks whilst paying no heed to the moderating influence of social context upon outlooks and behaviours, then I maintain that these are a poor guide to the social reality of people's thoughts and behaviours. When either a laboratory setting or an attitudinal survey is the favoured means to expose how individuals are most likely to think and act within the social dynamics of everyday life, then I tend to regard this as highly problematic. Where researchers adopt more ethnographic and/or qualitative approaches to data gathering and venture to consider the ways in which people's thoughts, feelings and behaviours vary from one social setting to the next, then it is generally the case that their findings serve, amongst other things, to cast a great deal of doubt upon claims made with reference to survey or laboratory research. As far as a proper *sociological* understanding of 'risk consciousness' is concerned, I hold that we have scarcely begun to piece together the full variety of ways in which this might be shaped, modified, amplified or attenuated within the social dynamics of day-to-day life.

Once again, in this setting, it might well be appropriate to cast sociology in the role of 'the awkward science', for while empirical sociological research offers discrete insights into the social processes that constitute people's cultural dispositions and routine behaviours, more often than not, it points to the conclusion that one would be ill-advised to offer any pre-emptive views on how people encounter risk in lived experience. At this level of research, sociology is inclined to highlight the extent to which knowledge of risk is always held *in process* as well as the *provisional* character of people's attitudes and behaviours towards phenomena labelled in these terms. The social world is a *dynamic* entity and our social being is constituted by cultural movements, interpersonal relationships and institutional pressures that are always liable to change. Here it may well be the case that sociological study is bound to raise the volume of debate over the limits of knowledge claims and the possibility of arriving at an adequate conception of society in lived experience.

RISK PERCEPTION RESEARCH

Most studies of risk perception are conducted within the field of psychology. Whilst working to solve problems arising within the technical domain of risk analysis, these are largely focused upon the effort to expose people's common-sense approaches to *the estimation of probabilities*. For the most part, psychological studies of risk perception do not engage in debates over the cultural formation of moral character or the general direction of social change, but, rather, are preoccupied with 'scientifically' documenting the ways in which individuals *visualise*, *encode* and *mentally process* information relating to a select range of 'natural', 'social' and 'technological' hazards. They tend to be concerned with the rule of thumb measures or 'mental heuristics' by which individuals cast judgements upon the magnitude of possible dangers and calculate the likelihood of experiencing harm. On this account, the meaning of risk is set as a form of mathematical reasoning. The tone of writing is designed to appeal to standards of 'scientific rigour' and the generally stated aim is to acquire an 'objective' (i.e. politically neutral) understanding of the cognitive techniques by which individuals work at presenting 'rational' explanations for their estimations of risk.

It is possible to group the psychological work on risk into at least three distinct bodies of research: (1) the 'heuristics approach', which is otherwise known as the 'psychometric paradigm'; (2) the 'optimistic bias approach'; and (3), studies investigating 'the impersonal impact hypothesis'. Each community of scholars can be distinguished according to the ways they prioritise their interests and represent the leading questions of their field. Here I offer a brief synopsis of the problems featured and advances made in each case.

The psychometric paradigm

'The psychometric paradigm' is probably the best-known body of psychological research on risk and is heavily associated with the work of Paul Slovic and his various collaborations (Slovic 2000). Drawing inspiration from Amos Tversky and Danny Kahneman's earlier research on the cognitive biases and mental heuristics that govern individual approaches to probabilistic thinking (Tversky and Kahneman 1974), Slovic and colleagues have put a considerable amount of effort into documenting the taken-for-granted assumptions that appear to determine the ways in which 'laypeople' perceive technological risk. The presentation of this work tends to be structured around a comparison between 'expert' assessments of various technological risks and 'lay' perceptions of their relative chances of being negatively affected by those risks. On this account, the 'objective' dimensions of risk are set in accordance with official records of annual accident and fatality rates associated with a host of risky behaviours and technological interventions. These 'objective' measures of risk are then compared to laypeople's intuitive perceptions of risk, with research being focused upon the task of explaining the discrepancies between the former and the latter. The overriding aim is to contribute to the development of a more scientifically 'rational' consensus with regard to the reality of the risks we face.

Individuals may be asked to categorise and estimate risks in various ways, but most research follows the 'classic' design of the earliest studies by requiring them to judge the severity of a particular type of risk according to scales indicating the extent to which it evokes a sense of 'dread', is judged to be 'known' or 'unknown', is perceived to be 'new' or 'old' or is assessed as 'voluntary' or 'involuntary'. Researchers typically find that while expert assessments of risk are in line with evidence presented by technical estimates of annual fatalities, lay judgements tend to be heavily influenced by factors beyond the actuarial domain. In contrast to the expert focus upon actual numbers injured or killed to date, lay perspectives on risk tend to pay more heed to the catastrophic potential of hazards, the threat posed by a particular technology to future generations and possibilities of exerting any measure of control over decisions that bring risks to society. These differences between expert assessments and lay perceptions of risk are particularly marked in the case of technologies associated with the nuclear and chemical industries. Psychometric researchers have consistently found that while experts categorise the risks associated with nuclear power and chemical processing plants as extremely low when compared to those of most other social activities and technological practices, laypersons tend to identify these as among the most dreadful and unknown of risks (Slovic 2000).

Such findings are understood to reveal that most people are not very good at estimating probabilities. However, researchers such as Slovic are not so crude as to label the typical layperson as 'irrational' or 'phobic'; rather, an explanation for this point of fact is developed in terms of an analysis of the mechanics of cognition alongside a critical focus on the quality of information about risk made available to individuals within the public domain. Accordingly, lay perceptions of risk are understood to be both a product of the mental heuristics that are typically deployed in everyday life to deal with risky situations and a result of the 'stigmatised' ways in which matters of technological and scientific risk are portrayed in news media (Heimer 1988; Flynn et al. 2001). On these grounds, it is argued that experts in the field of risk communication must both work at correcting 'inaccuracies' in the portrayal of scientific technologies in the public realm and, at the same time, find ways to present 'the truth' of matters that are in tune with our intuitive capacities for processing such information. The overriding contention here is that it is possible to bolster the scientific rationality of popular understandings of the social costs and benefits of modern technologies, but this requires governments and scientists to concentrate their attentions upon improving the quality and production of public information about risk (Slovic 2000; Powell and Leiss 1997). However, on this matter it is also important to note that few are prepared to place much confidence in existing practices of risk communication as the ideal means to achieve this goal. The hopes invested in public education as the immediate 'solution' to problems of risk perception are not matched by any good evidence to suggest that this is the most positive and reliable means to bring about major changes in individual's expressed thoughts and feelings about technological hazards (Fischoff et al. 1995; Jallinoja and Ayro 2000; Leiss 1996; Scholderer and Frewer 2003).

More recently, the attentions of Slovic and colleagues have turned to the moderating role played by emotions within judgements of risk. In this context, they have been interested to establish the ways in which an 'affect heuristic' 'motivates' the ways people reason about risky decisions (Althakami and Slovic 1994; Finucane et al. 2000). So far, major findings have concerned the extent to which judgements about risk appear to be structured by the quality and intensity of the negative feelings that individuals hold towards potential hazards. Moreover, in working to understand precisely how such feelings are acquired, the suggestion has been raised that societies develop a common 'affective pool' of evaluative responses to risk, but, to date, no serious research has been conducted into the conditions by which such a phenomenon is established and sustained. Ultimately, however, this research aims to piece together a more precise account of the interrelationships between cognition and affect, so as to arrive at a clearer understanding of how feelings might 'mislead' reason (Slovic 2000: xxxii–xxxiii); once again, the principle objective is to enable the development of a more scientifically informed cross-societal understanding of technological risks that promotes a greater consensus with regard to their relative costs and benefits.

The optimistic bias approach

The various works that can be grouped together as examples of 'the optimistic bias' approach share in some of the basic interests of the psychometric paradigm; namely, a commitment to understanding the ways in which our mental capacities for estimating probabilities may be rendered 'deficient' by the intuitive rules of thumb that govern everyday perceptions of risk. However, there is a major difference between these two approaches when it comes to the particular types of cognitive 'errors' that they aim to explain. Where the focus of the psychometric paradigm is firmly fixed upon the task of understanding 'laypeople's' psychological disposition to *overestimate* the risk of harm and exaggerate the catastrophic potential of various forms of technology, by contrast, 'the optimist bias' approach is more concerned to highlight the ways in which individuals are inclined to *underestimate* risks to themselves as compared to the ways in which they perceive risks for others. A key matter for concern here is the discovery that while people may well be inclined to judge risks to be high *for society*, they are far less likely to identify themselves to be *personally* at risk. In individual minds, societal level and personal level judgements about risk are held apart; where an individual may express a great deal of pessimism with regard to the risk-related prospects of society in general, they are far less likely to associate themselves with such a judgement. Indeed, researchers tend to be particularly concerned to highlight the ways in which the majority of individuals tend to be overly *optimistic* when it comes to assessing their own chances of avoiding harm.

While a great deal of psychometric research concerns the disjunctions between expert assessments and lay perceptions of risk in connection with the technologies of the nuclear and chemical industries, researchers with an interest in optimistic bias have tended to be more concerned with everyday risks relating to matters of health and safety (McKenna 1993; Taylor 1989; Taylor and Armor 1996; Weinstein 1980, 1982). For example, it has featured as a means to explain why individuals, despite being informed about the risks of contracting sexually transmitted diseases, still fail to practise safe sex (Sheeran et al. 1999; Taylor et al. 1992). Considerable disagreements remain as to how one should interpret the psychological significance of this finding. Optimistic bias has been attributed to 'information processing errors' connected with people's lack of personal experience with particular hazards, as evidence of the existence of an 'illusory' sense of control over one's life chances, as an illustration of the moderating force of negative affective states on individual capacities for estimating probabilities, and, further, as a sign of self-efficacy which under most ordinary circumstances is a positive sign of mental health (Weinstein 1987; McKenna 1993; Helweg-Larsen and Shepperd 2001; Taylor and Brown 1994; Weinstein and Lyon 1999). While it is a widely documented phenomenon, the psychological explanation for optimistic bias remains open to debate.

Along with a focus upon optimistic bias, researchers tend to be preoccupied with a set of 'managerial' concerns, which, again, are notably different to those of the psychometric paradigm. Where Slovic and colleagues have been concerned with the task of allaying people's apparently excessive anxieties concerning potentially catastrophic risks to society, for studies of optimistic bias the general aim is to find ways to make people *more* anxiously preoccupied with the personal risks they face. A great deal of this research takes place as part of health promotion campaigns, where the intention is to persuade people to adopt *precautionary* behaviours designed to improve their overall quality of life and prospects for longevity (Kreuter 1999). While studies of risk perception within the psychometric paradigm tend to debate processes of risk communication out of a concern to attenuate people's worries about technological hazards, for those with an interest in 'optimistic bias' a focus is placed upon the potential to provoke people to worry more about what they can do to avoid potential hazards; the major difficulty here concerns the art of persuading individuals to take measures to minimise their personal risk of harm. The point on which researchers all agree is that established procedures of risk communication fail to match with their ambitions; either in opposition to or in support for cultures of precaution, experts remain frustrated by the extent to which public perceptions of risk resist technical 'management' and change.

The impersonal impact hypothesis

Research conducted into the 'impersonal impact hypothesis' is largely concerned with debating the influence of mass media upon individual perceptions of risk. A key point of reference here is an article published by Tom Tyler and Fay Cook which presents findings from a series of studies exploring the impact of media representations of crime upon individual judgements about the risk of criminal victimisation, so as to argue that the majority of people tend to separate risks to society from risks to themselves, and that whilst mass media influence people's perceptions of societal risks, they are unlikely to have much impact upon the ways people make judgements about personal risks (Tyler and Cook 1984). Accordingly, these researchers share in an understanding of risk perception that features prominently within the optimistic bias approach; namely, that whilst individuals may perceive risks to society as dramatic and severe, when it comes to the perception of risk to themselves, then they are unlikely to associate themselves with the judgements they hold for society at large. However, a key difference is that whilst in the optimistic bias approach the focus of research remains fixed firmly upon the task of understanding the adaptive mechanics of human psychology, in most studies of the impersonal impact hypothesis attention is brought to bear upon the dynamics of a communication process in which individuals are held to interact with many spheres of influence besides mass media. A step is made towards thinking about individuals as social beings faced with competing demands for their attention and interacting in environments that are always liable to change.

Later studies have found a considerable amount of evidence to confirm the earlier hypothesis raised by Cook and Tyler, and beyond issues relating to criminal victimisation it appears that most people dissociate themselves from media reports on a broad range of health problems as well as matters of national economy and social security (Joslyn and Haider-Markel 2002; Mutz 1992; Park et al. 2001). However, at the same time a considerable amount of complexity has been brought into this framework of understanding. Most notably, attempts have been made to incorporate propositions relating to 'media system dependency'. It is argued that whilst the impersonal impact hypothesis holds true in the majority of instances, there are occasions where mass media may move individuals to dwell more deeply upon the extent to which their personal circumstances are entwined with broader social concerns. For example, when studying the influence of mass media upon the ways in which Australians assessed their chances of developing skin cancer, Thomas Morton and Julie Duck contend that mass media are more likely to have an impact upon personal beliefs when individuals rely more upon newspapers than television for their news and also when individuals set about interacting with mass media with the express purpose of gathering health information (Morton and Duck 2001). These researchers open the door onto questions about the relative importance of different kinds of mass media within people's cultural experience of everyday life, the particular ways in which they are used to satisfy a range of needs, the amount of concentration and effort that is required from media audiences in order to access information, and the culturally situated values that surround particular forms of print and broadcasting media across and within societies.

Studies of the impersonal impact hypothesis introduce a more sophisticated approach to understanding the influence of mass media upon risk perception than that which simply equates the content of media messages with public opinion. There are numerous studies of risk in the media that concentrate almost exclusively upon the task of interpreting the content of media messages under the naïve assumption that this provides some kind of a window into the hearts and minds of the majority of people in society (Flynn et al 2001; Pidgeon et al. 2003; Powell and Leiss 1997).

Others suggest that the salience of risk as a topic of social concern in everyday life grows in correspondence with the amount of space devoted to problems of risk in the mass media. Whilst research into the impersonal impact hypothesis proceeds under the assumption that the majority of people are able to recognise and comment upon risks to society, at the same time, it holds back from identifying people's social commentary with the preoccupations of their personal lives. When approached by researchers, the majority of people may be willing to offer a perspective on large-scale risks that appear in the daily catalogue of news; however, on this account, we should never venture to assume that individual opinions on problems *for society* have any bearing upon the worries and concerns of everyday life.

As in the case of 'the psychometric paradigm' and 'optimistic bias approach', studies of 'the impersonal impact hypothesis' tend to be geared towards the goal of offering a technical fix for the more effective 'management' of public perceptions of risk. As a basic point of understanding, it is accepted that this is not easily achieved. Whilst proceeding with the understanding that, in the majority of circumstances, most people split their attention between societal and personal risks so as to dissociate themselves from risks to society, critical attention has come to focus on the task of identifying the specific circumstances under which it still might be possible for a media message to intervene within this normal trait of human psychology so as to connect the personal with social. This brings psychology to the brink of debating with the bearing of social context and cultural environment upon individual differences in risk perception, but as we shall see, this only begins to touch upon the complexity of the research problems at hand.

THE IMPORTANCE OF SOCIAL CONTEXT

Psychological studies of risk perception serve to underline the fact that there is a considerable variety of ways in which individuals interpret and respond to information about risk. At the very least, they cast suspicion on any uniform account of public attitudes and opinion, but beyond that, I doubt that they provide us with much insight into the experience of risk in everyday life. In the majority of instances, this kind of research is conducted with the aim of providing policy makers with a 'magic bullet' solution for problems of risk communication. When it comes to bridging the gap between scientific assessments and public perceptions of risk, the task of research is directed towards the possibility of devising a means to discipline people's thought processes so that these bend in the direction of expert opinion. The largely unquestioned assumption here is that social attitudes and behaviours are the result of *individual* modes of cognition and innate dispositions of personality. People are conceptualised as rational agents, albeit with 'bounded' capacities for calculating the relative costs and benefits of their value-judgements and actions (Gaskell et al. 2004; Morgan et al. 2001; Jaeger et al. 2001).

Whilst psychological research tends to explain risk perception as a matter of brain function or personal aptitude, by contrast, sociologists bring emphasis to the ways in which our understandings about risk are shaped by social environments of everyday life. Rather than explore the mental processes by which individuals calculate probabilities, sociologists focus upon the ways in which social relationships in specific institutional settings influence the ways in which people experience and talk about their knowledge of risk. On these terms, knowledge of risk is always conceptualised as a matter of *social representation*, and in order to piece together an adequate understanding of how people are inclined to make sense of risk, we should be focusing our attentions on the dynamics of social thought and practice.

Most sociological studies of risk either concern people's attitudes towards environmental hazards or experiences of health issues. Whilst there are some important differences to be drawn between the problems featured in these fields, in both cases it is often the case that sociologists discover people to be thinking and feeling about risk in ways that defy expert anticipations. For example, in a much-cited study of farmers' approaches to managing the uncertainties of their working lives, Brian Wynne highlighted the ways in which expert assessments of risk were exaggerated as a result their ignorance of the routine practices of animal husbandry (Wynne 1996). In this instance, scientific experts assumed that both sheep and farmers behaved in ways that never featured in everyday practice, and, further, tended to denigrate farmers experience of work so as to privilege their own theoretical models of the 'reality' of risk. Wynne argued that over many years of dealing with testing environmental conditions and managing the contingencies of livestock rearing, farmers tended to be more alert to the hazards of their work than scientists were able to anticipate. In so far as experts failed to recognise these 'lay' experiences as scientifically valid, they conducted their experiments with models of working practice that bore no resemblance to the real world.

The potential for research in social context to reveal major discrepancies between expert and lay views on risk has been further highlighted on many occasions by sociologists working in the fields of health and medicine. Typically they find that while health professionals tend to work at communicating health risk with a technical understanding of the costs and benefits of clinical procedures, by contrast, patients interpret and respond to the information they receive in terms of moral feelings relating to experiences of social role and self-identity (Jones, D. S. 2008). Accordingly the social meaning of particular risks is often far removed from the bounds of probabilistic thinking, and, rather, is framed in terms of cultural meaning and affect (Warner 2008). For example, in studies of the ways in which women in their forties respond to genetic counselling sessions that cover the risks of 'being old and pregnant', Mette Henriksen and Bob Heyman discovered that it was largely through popular understandings of 'age-appropriate behaviour' that women reasoned with information relating to epidemiological risk. They also found that it was in relation to their respondents' capacities for coping with anxieties relating to their social responsibilities as older pregnant women that they arrived at the point of deciding whether to court the risks of miscarriage associated with amniocentesis (Henriksen and Heyman 1998). On this account, the interpretation and response to risk was considerably removed from purely cerebral negotiations with matters of statistical quantification. Here the meaning and experience of risk was largely emotional and the intensity of feeling seemed to be moderated by cultural outlooks on aging and motherhood.

An emphasis on the affective dimensions risk is also found in Nina Hallowell's study of the ways women negotiate with the knowledge of the likelihood of developing hereditary ovarian cancer (Hallowell 2006). Here she complains about the ways in which the representation of human experience in terms of risk tends to 'sanitise' lived experience. As a rational–technical language, she contends that the conceptualisation of ovarian cancer in terms of risk falls a long way short of capturing the emotional turmoil experienced by women living with the burden of knowing the physical and familial costs of developing this type of cancer. Hallowell argues that if we are truly committed to understanding the ways in which individuals negotiate with information concerning the possibility of future suffering and loss, then we should recognise that an exclusive focus on risk often renders the social world opaque to sociological understanding, for it fails capture the fear, anger, frustration and sadness with which the women in her study encountered and endured expert assessments of their life chances.

Hallowell's study also highlights the potential for matters such as gender and age to determine the ways in which individuals negotiate with the lived reality of risk. In social contexts of everyday life, social variables of class, age, ethnicity, gender, nationality and locality all appear to exert an influence upon individual modes of cognition, feeling and behaviour (Cutter 1993: 24–8). Indeed, one might well argue that if studies of risk perception pay no heed to the socio-demographic characteristics of their sample groups, then they have scarcely begun the work of piecing together the contingent factors that shape people's outlooks on life.

The point is well illustrated by Alan Irwin and colleagues in their study of the ways in which people living in the town of Jarrow perceive risks to the environment. These researchers emphasise that people's understandings of risk are always in the process of being negotiated and modified in relation to shifting contexts of everyday life. Their respondents' accounts of risks associated with a local chemical company varied according to the situations in which they were interviewed in and in relation to shifting terms of conversation about work and family life. Everyday understandings of risk were held as part of a dialogical process in which individuals expressed a considerable range of views, and there was often a high degree of incommensurability between expressed opinions as the terms of conversation shifted from one context to another. In this instance, the ways in which people talked about environmental risks varied according to whether they were in the company of work colleagues, with members of family at home or out with friends at the local pub. Aside from discovering the 'heterogenous character' of popular understandings of risk in everyday life, these researchers note that whilst working to draw conversation towards views on hazards associated with chemical pollutants, their respondents seemed to be more preoccupied with problems of employment, housing, crime and the quality of their children's education. Accordingly, Irwin and colleagues advise that risk researchers should be alert to the possibility that publics hold quite different views to those of experts when it comes to deciding which risks are most worrisome, and they might even find that most regard issues relating to risk as not worth worrying about as a day-to-day concern. It may be the case that it is only at the point where experts cue people to offer their opinions on risk that they actually give this matter their fleeting attention. In many instances, it may be only on the rare occasions when individuals engaged as respondents in a survey or interview setting that risk per se is called to mind.

THE PROBLEM OF SOCIOLOGY FOR RISK RESEARCH

In one of the first attempts at summarising the contribution of social science to our knowledge of how people perceive and respond to risk, Susan Cutter declares that the available evidence speaks more of our ignorance than understanding (Cutter 1993: 23). At the point of recognising the importance of factors such as race, gender and socio-economic status within the construction of people's outlooks on risk, she is left dismayed by the extent to which these matters remain on the margins of mainstream risk perception research. On Cutter's account, in their overriding concern to offer 'expert' advice on the task of shaping public opinion, researchers fail to grasp the full dimensions of the problem of establishing the *social reality* of people's thoughts and feelings about risk, and certainly are not in a position to inform our understanding of the relationship between perception and behaviour. She recognises that psychological risk research serves to document the rule of thumb measures that typify individual assessments of little known technological risks, but concludes that, insofar as it does not trouble itself with any inquiry into the ways in which people's thoughts and feelings vary and take shape in the multiple social contexts of everyday life, it should not be treated as a reliable guide to the reality of public opinion. Cutter calls for a greater involvement of sociology in the development of risk perception research so as to provide policy makers with data that are more sensitive to the social determinants of people's thoughts and behaviours.

Recent years have seen a number of moves to elevate the status of social science within risk research and some have even committed their careers to the project of promoting this as an inter-disciplinary field of study that marries sociology with psychology (McDaniels and Small 2004; Pigeon et al. 2003; Taylor-Gooby and Zinn 2006). With a largely uncritical adoption of the managerial ethos that characterises the research interest in risk, most of this writing is committed to highlighting social complexities that tend to be neglected within current terms of policy debate. Accordingly, having noted the ascendancy of psychometric studies within risk research and the expert preoccupation with managing public opinion, it is suggested that practitioners meet 'the challenge' of incorporating a range of sociologically informed insights within their models and procedures. It is argued that by attending to issues such as the social conditions that produce trust in institutions, affective responses to knowledge about risk and the occasions where people are attracted to the thrill of risk-taking, risk researchers are not only presented with opportunities for advancing new avenues of inquiry but also with insights that will augment the ways in which risks are theorised and studied (Zinn and Taylor Gooby 2006). The overriding assumption here is that whilst institutionally committed to distinct traditions of inquiry and operating with different analytical and methodological problems in mind, nevertheless, it is possible for risk researchers to complement one another's work; indeed, it is anticipated that practitioners are ready to accept that their working practices will benefit from a process of inter-disciplinary dialogue and collaborative study. The field of risk research is represented as a broad church whose members are committed to solving the same set of problems. The principle task at hand is portrayed as one of building bridges across the disciplines whereby each might benefit from the insights of others. The extent to which this requires practitioners to ignore long-established disciplinary schisms and tread lightly around traditions of epistemological dispute and methodological disagreement is hardly raised as a matter of concern.

Arguably, when it comes to sociology, those working within the field of risk research are more involved with a project of appropriation than a process of open negotiation and exchange. It favours the adoption of sociology as a means to provide nuance and detail to established traditions of risk research so that a limited role is accorded to processes of social construction within the formation of public opinion. The overriding interest is in a form sociology tailored to managerial concerns – a sociology that highlights opportunities for refining strategies of risk communication and suggests ways of designing policies to fit an ever-expanding portfolio of governmental problems.

For example, in an attempt to fashion a conciliatory footing for an engagement between risk research and sociological studies of risk in social context, Andy Alaszewski has worked harder than most to highlight the positive benefits of the latter for the former (Alaszewski 2005; Alaszewski and Horlick-Jones 2003). With a focus on the task of risk communication in clinical consultancy and health promotion, he contends that by working to understand the moral texture of people's interpersonal relationships and social aspirations, doctors might build relationships of trust with their patients so that opportunities arise for sharing health information in a process of reciprocal exchange. Alaszewski makes clear that on these terms the pursuit of risk communication as a 'technical fix' appears unlikely to deliver on its promise. Pointing to the examples of failed campaigns to persuade young people to stop smoking and to practise safe sex, he also argues that the pursuit of effective strategies of risk communication should question the notion that individuals generally behave as rational agents weighing up the costs and benefits of their health behaviours. Alaszewski's proposals are framed as a modest plea for person-centred strategies of communication and for institutional investments in relationships of trust, although this is couched with the invitation that researchers debate with the logics of many 'expert' approaches to risk communication.

Alaszewski does not explore the potential for the study of social context to bring more radical questions to bear upon the expert domain of risk debate. His interests lie firmly in applying sociology to current policy and practice so as to promote more effective measures of health care. His work does not seek to challenge the understanding that it is morally appropriate or politically desirable to categorise health problems and behaviours in terms of 'risk', or that studies of 'risk perception' and 'risk behaviour' deserve a high billing on the sociological research agenda. Alaszewski's project works to carve out a place for sociology *within* 'the risk debate'. He does not engage with forms of sociology that bring the ethical bearings of risk analysis into question. Such work turns a blind eye to debates relating to the extent to which the study of risk is disciplined by ideological interests. On this account, there is no place for critical sociologies that draw attention to the relationship between power and language and certainly there is no concern to engage with reflexive sociologies that encourage debate over the social conditions of knowledge production; yet, arguably, it is precisely with an interest in this level of analytical engagement that researchers work at attending to the meaning of risk in social context.

Whilst all the studies outlined in the preceding section tackle issues at the heart of risk research, or at least were initiated with that purpose in mind, they are all brought to the point of questioning the sociological legitimacy of risk. Through the experience of gathering their data, they are left wondering whether people's everyday thoughts and feelings about the problems they face are adequately expressed and accounted for when risk is privileged as the key issue at hand. It appears that too many social phenomena and experiences are left sidelined, sanitised or silenced when managerial and policy dimensions of risk are foregrounded as the primary concern. Such work moves beyond the mere suggestion that experts recognise the contribution of everyday concerns and feelings to the modes of cognition with which people make sense of uncertainties and risks; rather, on the understanding that technical matters of risk do not occupy a prominent place in people's lives at the level of everyday thought and feeling, it raises the critical contention that the analysis of risk may often obscure more than it reveals about the social character of lived experience.

On these terms, it can be argued that the study of risk in social context raises the possibility that, albeit with no malice of forethought, researchers perpetrate acts of 'symbolic violence' when they make no effort to reflect upon the ways in which the concept of risk emasculates the vitality of human experience (Bourdieu 1999). It might be suggested that in so far as researchers are unwavering in their commitment to analyse people's experiences and problems in terms of risk, then they deny opportunities for recognising and attending to the lived reality of human afflictions and anxieties. In the act of translating human experience into the cultural grammar of risk analysis and policy debate, researchers may be colluding in a process whereby the everyday languages, modes of expression and bodily experiences with which people negotiate with life's problems are not recognised as a matters worthy of wider attention and concern.

In recent times, where researchers work at observing and documenting people's attitudes and behaviours in social context, they have often expressed anxieties over the extent to which a 'crisis of representation' pervades social science (Atkinson and Coffey 1995; Gill 1998). The experiencing of meeting and talking with people in real-life situations, particularly where this presents opportunities for documenting experiences in everyday languages, has a tendency to make social researchers more sensitive to the ways in which academic discourse serves to muffle and mask lived reality. Researchers have been troubled by the extent to which the process of translating the experience of everyday life into scientific concepts and rational terms of analysis not only serves to fix unnecessary limits upon our fields of inquiry, but also leaves experts puzzling over problems that scarcely feature as prominent matters for concern in most people's day-to-day lives. This brings critical thought to the ways in which representations of social reality are inevitably tailored to select frames of cultural reference, and how these in turn favour particular moral and political perspectives on the world. On these terms, in a movement that repeats the earlier concerns raised by the political philosopher Hannah Arendt, attention is directed to the ways in which expert accounts of human trials and tribulations work to 'explain away' the details of lived experience so that these are treated (if at all) as only a trifling matter or peripheral concern (Arendt 1968).

This is the more radical level of debate raised by the study of risk in social context. It questions whether risk per se should be treated as a privileged focus of study. Such research works to unsettle moves to promote risk as an inter-disciplinary totem and common unit of analysis, or at the very least, it raises the volume of debate over the sociological value of risk when applied to the task of conceptualising human thought, feelings and behaviours. Certainly, it brings a moral and political frame to bear upon risk debates, so that methods of analysis and writing practices are examined in terms of their institutional biases and ideological bearings. Whilst some would confine sociology to the role of elaborating upon policy and managerial problems set by experts in risk analysis, it is often the case that the sociological study of people's attitudes and behaviours in social context raises methodological problems that, if taken seriously, have the potential to undermine the logics and conventions of a great deal of risk research. The experience of gathering research data in social context serves to direct critical attention towards the methodological means by which the knowledge of social science is produced and brought to the level of policy debate. Here it is not so much the case that sociology augments the expert study of risk, but, rather, that sociology becomes a problem for risk research.

CONCLUSION

In this chapter I have provided an overview of the ways in which experts approach the task of understanding what people think and feel about problems of risk. This requires a careful weighing up of the strengths and weakness of contrasting disciplinary interests and methodological concerns. In particular, it directs critical attention to the differences between sociology and psychology and the methodological compromises that allow for these disciplines to be married around a shared concern with the managerial dimensions of risk policy and strategies of risk communication.

How much do we know about the everyday realities of risk perception and behaviour? There is no agreement as to the best way of answering this question. Whilst a large amount of research is devoted to understanding how people think, feel and act in response to different kinds of information about risk, there is no consistency in approaches to research design, data collection and analysis. The task of piecing together an understanding of the methodological issues at stake across multiple fields of inquiry is complicated by the fact that the majority of publications are tailored more to appeal to sectional interests than to provide a critical appraisal of the evidence upon which knowledge claims are advanced for debate.

It is certainly the case that one is likely to find a number of different approaches to conducting sociological inquiries into the lived experience of risk. I have brought my narrative to a focus on studies that favour qualitative methods of inquiry and take a particular interest in the ways people use the language of risk and negotiate with its meaning in social contexts of day-to-day life. I have argued that studies of risk in social context tend to cast a great deal of risk debate and risk communication policy in a negative light; for time and again, the model of people as rational actors that is widely incorporated in expert risk research is made to appear as no more than a castle in the air. The textures and flows of thought and feeling in social context that are moderated through the diverse roles and identifications that people occupy and experience under conditions of everyday life are not grasped by modelling techniques that conceive of individuals as information processors and calculating machines.

At the very least, the *social* reality of risk perception is considerably more complex, uneven and ambiguous than many experts in risk analysis and risk communication hold to be the case (Bellaby 1990; Irwin et al. 1999; Tulloch and Lupton 2003). I contend that this finding has radical implications. It can be argued that by working to disclose the reality of risk perceptions and behaviours in social context, sociology works to problematise risk research. It is not just the case that sociological research draws attention to details and complexities that raise new problems for policy debate, but also that it records experiences of everyday life that fall outside the interests and concerns of a great deal of risk research. Here sociological research calls attention to the extent to which the public salience of the language of risk and its adoption within terms of policy debate may be more as a result of its value as a tool of ideology than its potential for sociological illumination. In many instances sociology raises the troubling suggestion that the privileging of the concept of risk as a means to label social problems and analyse the social world obscures more than it reveals about everyday trials and tribulations and the character of lived experience. It brings debate to the possibility that where problems of risk occupy the centre of inter-disciplinary debate, then this may be more because of willingness on the part of social scientists to analyse the world in terms of risk than a proportionate response to the ways in which risk has become a common currency of exchange in everyday life.

5

THE DANGER OF RISK

Sociologists have often taken an interest in the part played by ideology within institutional formations of society and broader dynamics of social change. The social and cultural means by which power is exercised in society is featured as a mainstream sociological concern. Certainly, both in works of theory and in the conduct of empirical research, many sociologists are concerned to address the moral and political interests at stake in the ways that symbolic forms of culture are used to bring social problems to our attention.

When outlining key components of 'the risk debate' in social science and contrasting sociological investments in these matters, I have taken opportunities to highlight the ideological bearings of the concept of risk. By linking the language of risk with the work of ideology I am suggesting that here we are not only presented with matters of cultural bias, but also with terminology that is used as a means to establish and sustain unequal power relations (Thompson 1990). The adoption of the concept of risk as a label for social problems, social attitudes and social behaviours promotes select ways of seeing the world. To call this 'ideology' incorporates the understanding that, in this cultural development, some interests are prioritised *to the cost* of others. I am lending support to the claim that the privileging of risk within our terms of analysis involves us either as unwitting accomplices or as willing agents in moral standpoints and political projects that produce social inequalities.

In earlier chapters, I argued that the sociological analysis of ideology tends to be muted within the expert domain of risk research. Whilst conceding that social factors have a moderating influence over individual modes of risk perception and encouraging the broader involvement of sociology within inter-disciplinary approaches to risk analysis, the expert field does not engage with sociological inquiries into the ways in which power relations are socially produced and institutionalised. Where priority is given to the management of public opinion, the administration of regulatory affairs and the promotion of health and safety measures, then it appears that very little encouragement is given to debates about the exercise of power in society. At the level of policy debate, risk research favours a technocratic brand of sociology, and in its devotion to advancing techniques for managing the ways people perceive and respond to risk, does not have much interest in questioning the moral values or political ideals advanced by its work.

It may well be as a result of an overriding commitment to refining instruments of rationalisation for regulatory practices and techniques of social control that, more often than not, the cultural theory of Mary Douglas is identified as the ideal means to bring sociological insight to the profession of risk management (Ball and Golob 1999; Hood et al. 2004; Jaeger et al. 2001; Royal Society 1992; Schwarz and Thompson 1990). Certainly, it appears that her framework of analysis readily complies with the logics set by the modelling techniques favoured by practitioners in this field, but, more importantly, it encourages a conservative stance in the conduct of social science. Indeed, Douglas herself admits that the organising principles of her theory lend support to the view that institutional arrangements governed by existing social hierarchies are best suited to the task of managing risk (Douglas and Wildavsky 1982: 196–8).

In so far as sociological theorists approach the analysis of risk out of a commitment to fashioning terms of social critique, then this is unlikely to feature in expert domains of risk research. Some perfunctory remarks might be directed towards the works of writers such as Ulrich Beck and Nikolas Rose, but, for the most part, researchers involved in detailing risk policy and augmenting techniques of risk management do not concern themselves with the critical aspects of their theories. While Beck and Rose aim to encourage the development of emancipatory movements of social change, risk research remains largely preoccupied with problems derived from the task of regulating and maintaining the institutional status quo.

It might also be as a result of the conservative character of their approach to social science that those working within the expert domain of risk research seem reluctant to engage with methodological questions relating to our capacity to provide an 'objective' account of the social world. It appears that whilst most empirical sociologists are prepared to engage with debates over the extent to which elements of subjective bias and personal interest influence the process of gathering and analysing research data, risk researchers tend to represent their work as dispassionate science. For the most part, the reflexive sociology that aims to expose the social practices and cultural dispositions by which academic fields set about the task of constructing knowledge of the world is not permitted to disrupt the conventions of risk research.

At various points throughout this book I have argued that, in terms of both their theoretical priorities and methodological practices, there are important distinctions to be drawn between sociology and risk research. Accordingly, I hold that it is important to recognise that, in so far as sociological research is tailored to the interests of risk research, it may well be the case that it is disciplined to a point where its critical potential is never allowed to take root and flourish. Where managerial concerns hold sway, little encouragement is given to debates that are geared to unsettle favoured interpretations of key concepts and no space is given to questions designed to unsettle the institutional priorities set for empirical research, and all the more so where this serves to cast the conduct of social science within an ideological frame. The 'sociology of risk' incorporates a competing range of theoretical narratives and many contrasting styles of research, but there are important differences to be drawn between the study of risk that takes place *for* sociology, and the 'sociological' work *of* risk research.

In this chapter I offer a critical sociology of risk. I question whether the concept of risk should be treated as a tool suited for the advancement of sociological understanding, or, rather, I outline a position that stands opposed to any move to privilege the analysis of risk where this sets limits upon the aims and scope of sociology. From the outset, I highlight the ideological potential and ramifications of the incorporation of risk discourse and risk analysis within the domain of sociology. I am particularly concerned to draw attention to some of the dangers associated with the privileging of the topic of risk in social science and wider realms of public debate. The first section features some of the moral and sociological concerns that might be raised along with the understanding that the promotion of risk analysis and risk assessment is linked to movements of intensifying processes of rationalisation. The second section explores the potential for risk discourse to serve as a cultural force of 'individualisation' so as to highlight the negative impact of this process on our political and sociological culture. The third section examines the kinds of issues that are prioritised as problems for risk debate and explores the possibility that these furnish us with an account of the social world that is blind to many of the risks that bring most harm to human life.

HAZARDS OF RISK RATIONALISATION

When outlining the semantic history of risk, I have already argued that it is useful to cast this as a component of wider processes of rationalisation. This brings attention to the cultural conditions and social pressures that dispose people towards probabilistic thinking in everyday affairs, the technologies that allow for the elaboration of techniques of rational control, and the institutional arrangements in which these acquire the political legitimacy and power to shape the wider dynamics of society. On many accounts, the advance of modernisation involves a systematic attempt to conform nature and society to the mandate of calculable rules, and from the outset, the development of methods of risk assessment and strategies of risk management can be identified as necessary components of this process.

Following seminal studies conducted by Max Weber into the cultural origins and fateful consequences of the modern drive to rationalise the world, sociologists have identified processes of rationalisation as a constant factor within the socio-cultural dynamics of modern societies and have continued to investigate how these impact upon our lives. On these terms, it is sociological common sense to depict modern science and technology as manifestations of particular tendencies and applications of rationalisation. It is also the case that sociologists understand processes of rationalisation to work at shaping modern administrative practices, production processes and bureaucratic procedures. Most sociological narratives on modern times devote discussion to the extent to which we are subject to cultural conditions that dispose individuals and institutions to adopt rationalising outlooks and behaviours. For sociology, processes of rationalisation are among the most powerful of the structural forces that govern our lives.

At the same time as Weber noted the efficiency of bureaucratic procedure, the accomplishments of modern science, and the potential for processes of rationalisation to 'master all things by calculation', he was also alarmed by the impact of these developments upon our humanity (Weber 1948d: 139). In his lecture on *Science as a Vocation* (1948e [1918]), he warned that technical rationality was unable to guide us in fundamental human concerns relating to the meaning and purpose of life; no doubt it advanced our practical and technical knowledge of the world, but it offered no adequate means to address questions of moral, aesthetic and human value. He linked the advance of rationalisation with a more pervasive sense of 'disenchantment', and while there is no overall agreement as to the details of Weber's theoretical investment in this term, it is widely understood that whilst relating this to the declining influence of religion in public affairs, he also identified it with a cultural outlook that held that the pursuit of human civilisation and progress was devoid of value and meaning.

Beyond reflections on the fate of metaphysics and the epistemological grounds for bestowing a moral value upon our humanity, Weber also claimed that when processes of rationalisation take hold of our social relationships and cultural outlooks, then it is likely that our appreciation for matters of fellow feeling and aesthetic accomplishment will diminish. He was deeply troubled by the understanding that along with the bureaucratisation of institutional and public life, an increasing amount of social and political power was landing in the hands of technical experts who were more interested in the exact execution of methodical conduct than in scrutinising the values and ends towards which this was directed. At the end of his second essay on *The Protestant Ethic and the Spirit of Capitalism* (1958 [1904–5]), he declares that the world is being taken over by 'specialists without spirit [and] sensualists without heart' and expresses his worries about the capacity for such people to set the standard for civilisation exclusively in terms of the discharge of official business (Weber 1958: 182). On this understanding, the discipline and mindset of bureaucratic officialdom operates 'without regard for persons'; its institutions are designed to operate as amoral machines (Weber 1948d: 215). People are liable to be treated in purely abstract terms – as numbers on a list where the overriding objective is to make all conform to the rule of calculation. Where the logic of institutional arrangements is set to pursue the maintenance of technical efficiency and order, our emotional being and individual circumstances are liable to be treated as trivial matters that hold no significant meaning, value or consequence.

Alvin Gouldner ventures to apply Weber's thesis to an analysis of our intellectual culture. He maintains that a 'new class' of intellectuals committed to the pursuit of purely technical ideals exerts an increasing amount of influence over the 'cultural grammar' of academic life (Gouldner 1978, 1979). Gouldner argues that this 'technical-intelli- gentsia' is inclined to regard a purely instrumental approach to managing social problems as the overriding purpose of 'modernisation', and on these terms, the humanistic credo of earlier generations of modern intel- lectuals tends to be given short shrift. It is now possible to devote an entire career to the refinement of technical–instrumental procedures for extending the bounds of rationalisation, and such interests tend to feature as a prominent concern within university course developments. Under these conditions we may find that while social science once attracted the attentions of ideologues, it is now increasingly disciplined to the interests of 'technologues'.

A number of writers identify the promotion of risk discourse in social science and public affairs as part of a movement to consolidate the tech- nocratic administration of academic research and policy debate, and at the same time suggest that it is because of the rise of an 'authoritarian technocracy' that problems of risk are featured so heavily in the public sphere (Beck 1995a; Healy 2001; Lofstedt 2005; Yeatman 1987). On these terms, the framing of social issues in terms of expert assessments of risk is perceived to offer few opportunities for questioning the democratic ethos and institutional practices of modern societies. Risk discourse is represented as the official language of institutions designed for the purpose of refining techniques of surveillance and social control (O'Malley 2004).

For example, with reference to recent developments in the research culture of Western medicine, John Arne Skolbekken maintains that the promotion of the language of risk can be understood as a consequence of the application of computing technologies to the gathering and analysis of probability statistics relating to health and illness (Skolbekken 1995). On this understanding, health care policy and clinical practice is being overtaken by 'surveillance medicine' (Armstrong 1995). The overriding purpose of health care is being defined in terms of technical procedures and regulatory practices for exercising greater measures of control over bodily behaviours and lifestyle choices. The interaction between health care professionals and their patients is conceptualised not so much in terms of a social exchange imbued with human sentiment and moral meaning, but more as a setting in which each is disciplined to comply with more rigorous regimes of rationalisation; the health care professional in the treatments they administer, and the patient in their compliance with the technical procedures and advice on offer. Certainly, there is no short-age of sociological research that exposes the social tensions and ethical dilemmas that arise for both practitioners and patients where techniques of risk assessment and regimes of risk management dictate the standards for health care practice (Hallowell 1999, 2006; Hallowell et al. 2004; Petersen and Wilkinson 2008; Sanders 2004; Savy and Sawyer 2008; Skillen et al. 2001). On many accounts it appears that where the rule of calculation sets the standard for clinical encounters and shapes the para-meters for health policy debate, then matters of personal feeling, cultural identification and social belonging are given short shrift.

Here the danger for sociology concerns the extent to which the adoption of the concept of risk as a tool of analysis and label for social problems represents the encroachment of an audit culture upon its field of interests and research practices. It may well be the case that the seman-tics of risk are so firmly rooted in conventions and cultures of rationalisa-tion that they militate against the possibility of aligning sociology with the pursuit of humane forms of society. Undoubtedly, it is the case that the language of risk is frequently identified with policies and practices that serve to silence and sideline issues of personal circumstance and fellow feeling. On a number of accounts it is suggested that where terms of risk analysis are favoured as a means to address social problems, then this serves to constrain the sociological imagination and deflect critical atten-tion away from questions relating to the nature of power relations in con-temporary societies (Rose 1999; Wilkinson 2006). If we treat seriously the concerns of writers such as Max Weber and Alvin Gouldner, then we might take the view that while the social character and consequences of risk debates are matters worthy of sociological interest, at the same time, they should not be privileged in any determination of the agenda for sociology.

THE NEGATIVE FORCE OF INDIVIDUALISATION

Contemporary societies are often depicted as comprised by social struc-tures and cultural movements that involve people in intensifying experiences of individualisation. Since the nineteenth century it has been frequently observed that, in so far as the quality of modern social life is shaped by increasingly complex divisions of labour allied to the spirit of capitalism, the advancement of consumerism and processes of urbanisation, then we should anticipate that most people will be disposed to think and act as distinct individuals. Under social conditions of capitalist modernity, it is widely held that individualism is a core component of the common-sense orientation to life. Following the foundational insights of writers such as Emile Durkheim, most accept that it is one of the few values and preoccupations that we now all share in common.

Sociologists tend to adopt a morally ambivalent attitude towards this development. Much sociological research is devoted to the struggle to understand the social circumstances in which individualisation works more to enhance than corrupt our personal and social well-being, but few venture to offer any firm prescriptions in this regard. It appears that whilst dealing with the difficulty of detailing the social dynamics of individualisation and its human effects, most shy away from the task of offering an opinion on how, if at all, this should or could be made to change. It is fashionable to represent individualisation as one of the more paradoxical components of modernisation (Honneth 2004). Majority opinion holds that while on many occasions it is experienced as a positive realisation of human freedoms; it can also be implicated in the development of aggravated states of anomie and socially corrosive attitudes of possessive individualism (Macpherson 1962). It is at once identified as a spur for the advance of humanism as well as a force that gives rise to a culture of narcissism.

On the positive side, individualisation is recognised as a potential force of liberation. The fact that modern people are immersed in social processes, cultural experiences and working practices that require them to negotiate with the direction and meaning of their lives is understood to increase existing possibilities for self-realisation. Many components of so-called 'traditional' ways of life are understood to be rooted in oppressive social structures that provide limited opportunities for acts of self-determination. In so far as individualisation gives rise to a shared passion for human rights, it is recognised as part of the social conditions that nurture the development of political campaigns opposed to racism, sexism and class privilege (Durkheim 1973). It is also possible to find commentators celebrating the individualising force of modern consumerism on the grounds that, at a popular level, it provides multiple avenues for self-expression (Fiske 1989). Albeit via a dependency on the medium of cash exchange, the spread of consumer culture is understood to provide historically unprecedented opportunities for exploring individual aesthetic tastes and interests on a massive scale (Simmel 1990).

On the other hand, processes of individualisation are frequently cast in negative terms as sources of high anxiety and as the succour to egoistic impulse. The experience of individualisation that is rooted in the disciplinary force of the capitalist marketplace upon our lives is often represented as a primary source of our social impoverishment and as a key factor within the development of egocentric attitudes and personalities (Putnam 2000; Lasch 1979). It is also the case that throughout the history of modernity, social commentators have lamented the extent to which the experience of living in individualised societies leaves large numbers of people feeling desperately alone and culturally ill-equipped to cope with their enforced states of autonomy (Fromm 1942; Riesman 1950). Under these conditions, the 'freedoms' afforded by consumerism tend to be represented not so much as an avenue towards human flourishing, but, rather, as a cultural pathology that dooms individuals to an insatiable quest for self-identity and social meaning (Veblen 1953).

At the very least, it is recognised that processes of individualisation involve us in 'precarious freedoms' (Beck 2002: 42), and, indeed, for theorists such as Ulrich Beck and Anthony Giddens, this further underscores the value of the concept of risk as a means to depict the presiding quality of social life in our times (Giddens 1990, 1991; Beck 1992). They hold that intensifying levels of flexibility in the workplace, particularly in the context of short-term contractual work, disposes individuals to approach paid employment in terms of a personal risk borne at the cost of unsettling experiences of insecurity and anxiety. The difficulty of securing paid employment in contexts of pronounced economic uncertainty is also identified as a force that erodes the quality of our personal relationships. Where partnerships and friendships fall apart it is often because of pressures of work that leave little space and time for nurturing ties of intimacy. On this account, the trials and tribulations of love and work are an integral feature of the 'risk society' (Beck 2000b; Beck and Beck-Gernsheim 1995; Giddens 1992).

In their concern to analyse Ulrich Beck's account of the ways in which the ecological hazards of industrialisation confront societies with an imperative to change, commentators tend to neglect the extent to which his thesis is comprised by an account of the ways in which everyday worries about work and family life are channelled into public issues relating to the portent of environmental catastrophe. Beck holds that in so far as populations are increasingly made to be economically, biographically and emotionally self-reliant, they are also more disposed to share in public anxieties over the future of the world. A heightened sense of vulnerability at home pours oil on the fires of worries about the overall fate of humanity and the natural world (Beck 1992: 127–38).

It is often assumed that a 'risk society' is also an 'individualised society'. In sociological narratives on our times, a great deal of the popular currency of risk appears to be related to the extent to which it serves an appropriate label to describe shared forms of social consciousness. At one level, the concept appeals to the understanding that large numbers of people are forced by social circumstance to assume responsibility for the course and direction of their lives. Where people find themselves with 'no choice but to choose' how to live within precarious social situations and unstable economic conditions, the labelling of attitudes and behaviours in terms of risk appears to be an apt way to describe the ways in which individuals square up to life (Giddens 1994, 1991). It is assumed that the everyday task of living in such societies requires an ever more refined ability to assess the personal costs and benefits of every thought and action. For when things go wrong, individuals are left with no one but themselves to blame, or, rather, these are the social conditions that shore up the 'common-sense' understanding that individuals should be held personally responsible for their fate.

However, it is precisely with reference to this 'common-sense' attitude that a number of critics identify some of the more insidious social applications of the language of risk. As I have already indicated when outlining the governmentality perspective in Chapter 3, some hold that it is not merely the case that the concept of risk serves as an apt way to describe components of the lived experience of individualisation, but also understand this to operate in the service of an individualising worldview. On this account, when the language of risk is used as a means to explain social problems and advise people on the course of action they should take to avoid coming to harm, it is often the case that authorities are involved in promoting the view that individuals should 'take upon themselves' the responsibility for managing their health and security. A political motivation is at work here; one that aims to have people embrace the view that individuals are in every way responsible for their well-being.

For this reason, Nikolas Rose regards the prominence of risk debate in contemporary societies as part of a cultural shift that heralds 'the death of the social' (Rose 1996). He argues that Western governments are abandoning the task of creating social institutions and economic conditions that promote social solidarity on a national level; the project of nation-building on behalf of the collective good no longer commands the logics of their administrative practices and governmental strategies. Rose claims that 'the territory of government' is being reconfigured by social policies designed to make individuals assume responsibility for their lifestyles and livelihoods. Such policies not only serve to make people attend to the risks they pose to others and themselves, but also sanction the official means to discipline individuals who 'pose a risk to the community on a account of their failure to govern themselves' (Rose 1996: 349). For Rose, the application of techniques of risk assessment and risk management to the logics and practice of government lends support to a political credo that holds no place for identifying the distribution of poverty, health inequalities and rates of crime as moral problems relating to the determining force of society upon our lives. The advent of risk discourse consolidates a worldview that locates the source of public problems in the attitudes and behaviours of discrete individuals.

It is particularly in relation to the analytical and political status of the concept of class that sociologists might recognise this development as cause for alarm. Whilst some might argue that the majority of people in Western societies no longer adhere to a strong sense of class identity, it is certainly the case that there is strong evidence to suggest that economic inequalities are widening within and between most societies across the world. Since the late 1970s there has been an ever-widening gap in the incomes of the rich and poor in most OECD countries (OECD 2008). For example, according to the United Kingdom's Office for National Statistics the average income of the top 20 per cent of households is now over fifteen times greater than that of the poorest 20 per cent; between 2006 and 2007 the average income of the richest quintile was £75,000 (falling to £52,400 after tax) whilst the average income for the poorest quintile was £4900 (rising to £14,400 after benefits) (Jones 2008).

It is important to recognise the human cost of such pronounced levels of inequality. The poor are not merely disadvantaged in terms of their consumer spending power, but, most significantly, in relation to their life chances, living conditions and life expectancy. It is well established that there is a consistent association between income inequalities and health inequalities (Chandola 2000; Kunst et al. 1998; Power et al. 2005). In Britain there is a significant social class gradient in childhood morbidity in the first ten years of life. When categorised in terms of the registrar general's class schema, children born into class group V have a rate of mortality that is 40 per cent higher than class group I (Petrou et al. 2006).

Children from more disadvantaged sections of society are more vulnerable to respiratory and gastrointestinal infection, middle ear disease and dental caries and they are also more likely to die in road traffic accidents (Reading 1997; Moynihan and Holt 1996; Woodroffe et al. 1993; Sharples et al. 1990). As adults, lower-income groups die more frequently from cardiovascular disease, coronary heart disease, stroke, lung cancer, stomach cancer, respiratory disease, accidents, violence and complications arising from the consumption of alcohol and use of drugs (Galobardes et al. 2004). A recent report by the World Health Organisation notes that while those living in one of the richest districts of Glasgow (Lenzie) have a life expectancy of eighty-two years, their neighbours living in the considerably poorer district of Calton have a life expectancy at birth of only fifty-four years. Such facts speak not only of radically contrasting levels of exposure to risk but also of extreme differences in the experience of harm (WHO 2008: 32).

There is research that brings support to the view that neo-liberal economic policies and governmental practices should be held responsible for still widening income and health inequalities, and that in countries such as Britain and the United States where such policies exert the greatest influence over the presiding welfare regime, these are now more pronounced than ever before in history (Coburn 2004; Leyland 2004). For this reason, if critics such as Rose are right to identify risk discourse as a component of the ideology of neo-liberalism, then at the very least we might be wary of the ways in which it is taken up as part of the language of sociology. Certainly it is the case that while there is evidence to suggest that relative experiences of class exert a significant influence over the ways individuals perceive the risks they face, there is scarcely any mention of this issue within expert domains of risk research (Cebulla 2007). In the majority of instances, social attitudes and responses to the problems featured in risk research are studied in terms of the ways in which aggregates of individuals perceive hazards, and, further, any assessment of harm is almost always conducted with 'the average individual' in mind.

Whilst it would be wrong to cast Ulrich Beck as a champion of neo-liberalism, it is perhaps disturbing to note the potential for his terms of analysis to lend support to the view that social problems should be addressed at the level of 'the individual'. At various points he argues that in order to understand the social experience of emergent forms of risk society, we would do well to abandon the analysis of class. Beck emphasises the ways in which the majority share in the same experiences of threat and uncertainty and how this in turn serves as the social ground upon which to 'reinvent' politics. He is inclined to celebrate the democratising force of the threats posed by large-scale industrial hazards, for he holds that worries over their potentially disastrous consequences transcend class and national boundaries. Beck argues that it is increasingly likely that both the rich and the poor will be forced to share in the burden of dealing with the human and environmental costs of industrialisation. Indeed, in later works he goes so far as to suggest that we should regard 'class' as no more than a 'zombie' concept – dead in the real world, and only treated as a 'live' issue in outmoded sociological textbooks (Beck 2000a; Beck and Willms 2004).

At no point does Beck moderate his arguments with any documentation of social distributions of the experience of harm. Whilst at one point referring us to the horrific chemical plant disasters at Bhopal and Villa Parisi (Cubatão) as evidence for the possibility that 'the multiplication of risks' will cause 'world society to contract into a community of danger', in subsequent publications he makes no attempt to assess this claim in relation to the ongoing record of human suffering (Beck 1992: 43–4). Certainly it is the case that in terms of health inequalities there is little evidence to suggest that there is much commonality in the lived experience of risk across the globe. Indeed, the available data points to extreme cross-national differences in the experience of debilitating physical and mental health problems. Where the richest sections of the minority of the world's population living in advanced industrial nations can expect to live to around eighty years of age, the majority of the world's population live in regions of the globe where life expectancy is between sixty and sixty-five years of age. It is often the case that in countries ravaged by HIV/AIDS and TB, the rate of mortality is so high that, at birth, life expectancy is around forty years of age or less (DESA 2007; Marmot 2005).

At face value, there is nothing inherently at work within the logics of risk that would lead one to identify this as the handmaiden of individualisation. Techniques of risk assessment and the language of risk could be used as part of the inquiries into the social conditions that cause damage to human life. The expert field of risk analysis could be refashioned so that the privileging of debates about the ways in which individuals negotiate lifestyle risks or perceive technological and chemical hazards is supplanted by a focus on the social determinants of material deprivation and harm. Debates about risk might well be raised not so much with a focus on how abstract individuals judge the reality of threatening circumstances, but more out of an interest in the ways in which the dynamics of economy and society are set in motion so that some groups are guaranteed to be more at risk of harm than others.

At present, one of the dangers for sociology lies in the extent to which the analysis of risk takes place so as to diminish one of the most distinguishing attributes of sociological thinking; namely, the understanding that people's thoughts, actions and bodily experiences are products of the social circumstances in which they are made to live. Properly conceived, sociology is always inclined to bring emphasis to questions relating to the determining force of social structures upon individual outlooks and behaviours. In this respect, it is out of a concern to understand the social conditions that allow for the flourishing of our individuality and with an interest in nurturing the forms of society that are most likely to provide us with the means to actively realise our human potential, that sociologists pursue their vocation. There is reason to question whether such matters have a place within the mainstream of current risk research, and there may be just cause to frame a great deal of this as a cultural development that hamstrings sociological thinking.

A QUESTION OF PRIORITIES

So far I have raised some critical questions relating to the moral values that influence the conduct of risk research. I have also worked to bring attention to the political beliefs that appear to moderate the conceptualisation of human experience in narratives on 'risk society'. I have been particularly concerned to pay heed to the possible limits that are set upon the terms of sociological inquiry when the language of risk is privileged as a means to study the social world. I have worked to sound some notes of concern over the ways in which the prominence of risk debate in public life and policy debate not only leads to a narrowing of the sociological imagination but also a retreat from sociological thinking.

In this final section, I aim to elaborate further on these matters by questioning the ways in which problems are prioritised in terms of risk. This already features as a topic of interest in a selection of articles published in journals devoted to the promotion of risk research (Ball and Golob 1999; Morgan et al. 2001; Sjoberg et al. 2005). In the expert domain, the task of ranking risks largely concerns the identification of criteria for upholding an 'objective' account of the probable occurrence of specific events of adversity. In its purest form this tends to be conducted with reference to official fatality and accident rates. However, it is also recognised that many of the issues that receive a high billing as 'problems' for the field are unlikely to occupy the interests or experiences of society at large.

For example, David Ball and Laurence Golob note that much risk research is devoted to the study of 'what if' questions relating to highly specialised industrial and technical processes where matters of occupational safety and commercial value are prioritised above any interest in views held by 'the general public' (Ball and Golob 1999: 245). Indeed, on more than one occasion it has been noted that the chemical and nuclear industries appear to exert an inordinate amount of influence over the agendas of research set for the field (Adams 1995; Freudenberg and Pastor 1992). A large number of articles are devoted to documenting the carcinogenic properties of specific chemicals, the risks involved in transporting various kinds of hazardous waste products and the best ways to dispose of the toxic by-products from industrial processes. Whilst experts are alert to the extent to which they appear to be overly preoccupied with risks relating to levels of radiation, the incidence of BSE and new biotechnologies, such matters continue to receive a high billing in specialist journals (Sjoberg et al. 2005).

Looking back over the last ten years of published articles in three of the most widely cited journals, *Risk Analysis*, the *Journal of Risk Research* and *Health Risk and Society*, one might well conclude that the topics that feature most prominently are more a result of the priorities set by funding agencies than a product of any impartial review of the hazards that place the largest numbers of people at risk of harm. In *Risk Analysis*, food risks relating to matters such as BSE-infected beef products, levels of mercury in fish and listeria contaminated cheese (92 articles) and health risks associated with various types of toxic chemicals (77 articles) receive the most attention; but risks connected with the threat of terrorism (42 articles), levels of radioactivity (36 articles), hazardous waste disposal (27 articles) and air-borne pollutants (24 articles) also receive a high billing. Food risks (19 articles) are also a headline concern in the *Journal of Risk Research* along with risks associated with biotechnology (20 articles), environmental health (20 articles) and the activities of the nuclear (11 articles) and chemical industries (10 articles). Both *Risk Analysis* and the *Journal of Risk Research* also feature large numbers of articles that are devoted either to methodological disputes in risk assessment and risk perception or to documenting the problems for risk management posed by the regulation of industry. Indeed, in many issues more articles are devoted to defending the credibility and legitimacy of particular methodological and managerial practices than to any other matter.

As a general rule, the articles published in *Health Risk and Society* are not so heavily concerned with defending the rigour of their science or promoting their managerial value to industry and government. There is some shared ground with *Risk Analysis* and the *Journal of Risk Research*, but, at the same time, the focus upon the conjunctions between risk and health care appears to provide room for featuring a broader range of methodological approaches and research agendas. This journal tends to attract more submissions from qualitative researchers, and alongside the usual interest in risk perception there is a greater concern with documenting the bearing of risk issues upon specific health behaviours and patient–practitioner interactions. In this context, problems relating to sexual health (17 articles), genetic screening (16 articles), mental health assessment (15 articles), food risks (12 articles) and illicit drug use (8 articles) get the most attention.

It may be argued that the range of problems featured in such journals should be welcomed on the grounds that they represent some productive avenues for sociological research and thinking. Certainly it is the case that it is through the rise of risk debate that many problems relating to the environment and public health have been brought within the sociological field. Risk issues have featured heavily within the rapid growth of the study of health and medicine as one of the largest fields of contemporary sociological research (Skolbekken 1995; Petersen and Wilkinson 2008). It is also very likely that most sociologists would identify the language of risk as a major component of movements to link the fate society with that of 'nature' and 'the environment' (Barry 1999; Goldblatt 1996; Irwin 2001; Strydom 2002).

At the same time, more dissenting voices have argued that we should be wary of the extent to which problems raised in the contexts of risk research represent not only a minority point of view on topics worthy of attention, but also one that is frequently marked by the interests of some of the most economically and political powerful sections of society. In an early sociological review of the field, William Freudenberg and Susan Pastor contend that sociologists should be particularly wary of the extent to which the priorities and methodological practices of risk research come under the influence of elite establishment concerns (Freudenberg and Pastor 1992). Indeed, they go so far as to suggest that, in many instances, specialists working within the technical domain of risk research are involved in projects where one group seeks to impose risks on others. On this account, sociologists should be careful to pay heed to the extent to which the agendas for risk research are determined by sectional interest groups that have no desire to pursue questions relating to who has the legitimate power to decide which risks should be prioritised and how issues of 'social benefit' and 'technological progress' should be defined.

At the very least it must be surely be conceded that the risk debate in contemporary social science largely concerns the interests and fates of sections of population in the most industrially advanced sectors of the globe. In almost every instance, narratives on 'risk society' and the preoccupations of risk research concern the experiences of populations located in the United States, Western Europe or Australia. In this regard, we only have a minority report on how or why matters of risk should be prioritised as problems for social science.

At one level this might be addressed as a matter that denies a proper understanding of the social dimensions and human costs of many of the hazards featured within established risk literatures. Whilst the risks posed to populations by the use of hazardous materials in industrial processes are generally assessed with reference to numbers of accidents, injuries and fatalities in developed nations, it is in developing nations that the highest numbers of deaths take place as a result of exposure to toxic chemicals. Weak legislative controls, rapid and disordered processes of industrialisation and the fact that many industrial plants are located in areas populated by large numbers of the most socially disadvantaged sections of society are some of the factors that combine to ensure that the hazardous potential of many technological risks is far greater in the developing world. In terms of the numbers of fatalities involving hazardous materials, India, Mexico, Russia, Brazil and China are the countries most deserving of the label 'risk society' (de Souza 2000). These are also the countries where the largest numbers of occupational accidents and fatalities take place. At a conservative estimate, when compared to United Kingdom and United States, the rates at which people are injured or killed in the workplace are at least three times higher in developing countries (Hämäläinen et al. 2006). It is also important to recognise that in the absence of adequate health care facilities, welfare provision or insurance facilities, the levels of collateral damage and harms caused by such events are far more extensive and acute than anything experienced in industrially advanced nations.

There is a more pressing issue to be raised here, for one might well contend that if the terms of risk debates were moderated in relation to the conditions responsible for global fatality rates, there should be a far more radical reordering of the priorities set for political attention and policy debate. In relation to the global burden of disease it is childhood and maternal malnutrition, unsafe sex, poor quality drinking water, inadequate sanitation facilities and the inhalation of indoor smoke from solid fuels that feature most heavily among the risk factors implicated in the destruction of human life. In developing contexts, it is the incidence of neonatal complications and diarrhoea along with diseases such as pneumonia, malaria, measles, tuberculosis and HIV/AIDS that lead to the most premature deaths (Ezzati et al. 2002; WHO 2002). On this evidence, the priorities set for contemporary risk research stand in stark contrast to the everyday experience of risk encountered across the globe.

In so far as most risk research is conducted without any priority being placed upon the harms caused by conditions of material poverty and social deprivation, one might well conclude that it is ill-suited to provide much insight into the true dimensions of a 'world risk society'. Many of the problems featured in the leading risk research journals are of a highly esoteric order and are only liable to concern tiny sections of populations in the most privileged sectors of the globe. Where problems are featured that threaten large numbers of people with some form of damage or harm, then the boundaries of concern tend to be set with the plight of advanced industrial nations in mind. In this regard, whilst matters such as 'the terrorist threat' attract increasing amounts of attention within the risk literature, at no point does any publication acknowledge the brute fact that more people die each day from the incidence of diarrhoea than were killed in the bombing of the twin towers on 9/11. My fear is that the priorities set for current risk research not only serve to cast a veil upon the suffering of vast swathes of humanity, but also render sociology irrelevant to the majority experience of life around the globe.

CONCLUSION

One of the presiding themes in my writing on the sociology of risk concerns the need to constantly question the ways in which the language of risk is incorporated within the depiction and analysis of social problems. I have argued that we should always be careful to pay heed to the political beliefs and moral values that are advanced when areas of social life and cultural outlooks are ring-fenced as matters for risk debate. I have worked to alert readers to the analytical premises and interpretive biases that tend to feature when the concept of risk is held up as a lens through which to study society and categorise human behaviours. At various points I have highlighted the ways in which the conventions of risk research serve to compromise the conduct of sociological research and curtail opportunities for critical sociological thinking.

In this chapter I have outlined some reasons for approaching the analysis of risk not so much as a positive development for sociology, but, rather, as a form of thinking and arena of study that works against sociology. In so far as public debates about risk and the promotion of risk research comprise movements to conform areas of social life to strictures of rationalisation, then sociologists should be alert to the ways in which this denies possibilities for recognising and addressing the more rationally incoherent components of human experience. Where we find the language of risk mobilised as part of narratives on society levelled at the ways in which 'the average individual' experiences the world, then sociologists should beware the extent to which this serves to withhold recognition from the brute facts about class inequalities and highly uneven social distributions of harm. If the priorities set for risk research are embraced as part of the agenda for the reformation of sociology, then those with any residual commitment to understanding the human costs of modernisation should be alarmed when this pays no heed to the lived experience of the poor majorities in the real world risk society.

Of course, my manner of writing and argumentation betrays a commitment to a particular form of sociology. I place a high value on the works of those who aim to be both critical and humanistic in their approach to studying the social world. My commitment lies in the nurturing of a sociology that pays heed to and makes known multiple forms of lived experience for the purpose of our collective social enhancement. I hold that the importance of sociology lies in the contribution it makes to the progressive reduction of social suffering and the creation of more humane forms of society. My fear is that the turn to risk in contemporary social science serves to divert attention away from these aims and diminishes their moral value.

6

OUR FUTURES AT RISK

In the process of writing this book I have felt increasingly uneasy about the extent to which many of the featured topics of debate have been superseded by recent world events. When set against the backdrop of a rapidly escalating global crisis in food production, unprecedented volatilities in world energy supplies and the meltdown of international financial markets, it is difficult to resist the conclusion that the current parameters of risk debate in social science are woefully ill-suited to the task of making sense of the urgent public issues of our times. It has become abundantly clear that in order to grasp the overriding dynamics of the world risk society, then problems relating to the availability and distribution of food, fuel and finance must be addressed as among the most pressing of all human concerns. While almost on a daily basis the global importance of these matters is underlined via ever-more disturbing reports on the human misery and social upheaval caused by rapidly escalating costs of living and economies in recession, it seems all too obvious that there is just cause to worry about the means to control food and fuel prices and preserve paid employment. In retrospect, it is shocking to note the extent to which the interrelationships between these problems have been neglected in mainstream sociology, and all the more so in domains that privilege the issue of risk.

A new world (dis)order is rapidly taking shape. A recent United Nations report on the current world economic situation comments that for many years the governments of advanced industrial nations have been warned that the years of sustained economic growth through the early 2000s were secured at a high level of risk (UN 2009). In retrospect, one of the most surprising aspects of the 2008 financial crisis may be identified in the extent to which it was greeted by politicians and policy makers as an unanticipated and bewildering event. It was already understood that a combination of easily accessible consumer credit, the wide availability of securitised mortgages and over-inflated house prices were liable to create conditions for economic disaster. For a considerable length of time it was also acknowledged that the growing trade deficit between United States and China was bound to exacerbate the volatilities of world markets, and all the more so when placed under the spur of heightened demands for energy use (Hung 2008).

The panic that swept through the world banking system as investors rapidly lost confidence in the value of securitised mortgages in the United States and created a liquidity crisis took place in the same period of a rapid increase in the price of oil. As they struggled to implement policies to re-capitalise markets and reform the mortgage industry, governments were also beset with the task of managing inflationary shocks to their economies wrought by the escalating costs of energy use. Whilst this inevitably added to the price of food, as part of the accounting for this development suspicions were also cast towards the increasing amounts of investment in crop-based bio-fuels and how this was impacting upon the availability and price of wheat, corn and rice. Further shocks to the world food production system came from the agricultural devastation caused by severe droughts and floods that many attributed to the cumulative impacts of global warming.

On the 25 April 2008, the Executive Director of the World Food Programme, Josette Sheeran, warned of a 'silent tsunami' sweeping the earth as global food prices rose by 55 per cent between June 2007 and February 2008. Over this period the global price of wheat rose by 130 per cent while the price of rice increased by 74 per cent. Food riots were recorded in Niger, Senegal, Cameroon and Burkino Faso and street protests took place in Mauritania, Ivory Coast, Egypt, Morocco, Yemen, Mexico and Italy. By the end of 2008 the UN Food and Agriculture Organisation identified thirty-six countries as requiring external food aid assistance in order to feed their populations (www. fao.org). The World Bank estimate that between 2003 and 2008 the number of malnourished people in the world rose from 848 million to 967 million, with 44 million being added during the 2008 food crisis (World Bank 2008).

While oil prices fell rapidly with the onset of a global economic recession, it is anticipated that they will soon be on the rise again. It may well be the case that we have already passed peak oil production and even according to the most optimistic forecasts it is predicted that oil production will rapidly decline from 2020 if not before (Deffeyes 2005; Heinberg 2007). The thirst for energy from China and India is likely to increase, thus guaranteeing future shocks to the price of fossil fuels; the political and economic volatilities derived from the pressure to maintain oil supplies along with the task of managing market speculation over the future of the energy industry are set to continue for the foreseeable future.

The scientific documentation of the adverse effects of climate change also lends support to the view that the cumulative crises of 2007–8 are but early warning tremors ushering in a new era of environmental disaster. The effects of increases in the temperature of the globe are being made clear in rising sea levels and more volatile weather patterns that guarantee the destruction of large components of the ecosystem. It is anticipated that the rate of environmental change does not leave sufficient time and space for managed processes of adaptation. The Intergovernmental Panel on Climate Change (IPCC) contends that we are now witness to mass extinctions in the natural world and that large sections of the world's population are living in latitudes that stand to be severely affected by extreme conditions of flooding or drought. It is already clear that these conditions are set to have a negative impact on crop production, and as a consequence it is highly likely that soon well over one billion people of the world's population will be malnourished. Where hundreds of millions of people now live in areas that are likely to be impacted by extreme water shortages or catastrophic flooding, the IPCC also contend that the global burden of diarrhoeal disease will rapidly increase (IPCC 2007).

Under these conditions the apocalyptic language that is frequently used by Ulrich Beck as a means to herald the advent of world risk society may be quite apposite. On a number of highly authoritative accounts we now inhabit 'a world of creeping catastrophe' where large sections of humanity are being alerted to the fact that they are living on 'a volcano of extinction'. It is, however, where Beck seeks to make clear the parameters of risk that his narrative is less suited to address the urgent demands of our times. Whilst he devotes considerable amounts of space to raising social alarms over the potential for the nuclear and GM food industries to precipitate a world ecological crisis, it is most likely the case that these will now be judged to be among the more benign factors that comprise the new era of disasters; indeed, nuclear energy may well be the only viable alternative to fossil fuels and GM foods might yet make a positive contribution to alleviating global food shortages. In contrast to Beck's thesis, the risks that have the greatest impacts upon people's lives relate to fundamental components of household economy and social conditions of family life and work. The real parameters of the world risk society are being made brutally clear in people's ongoing struggles to meet basic needs and/or sustain adopted lifestyles whilst searching for a means to protecting themselves against frequent shocks to the world economy wrought by the inherent wildness of the capitalist marketplace at a point in history where supplies of fossil fuels are in decline and climate change is precipitating a global ecological crisis.

One of the most sobering and detailed assessments of the large-scale risks poised by our current global predicament is provided by a Directorate General of the United Kingdom's Ministry of Defence that works under the title of the Development, Concepts and Doctrine Centre (DCDC). When put to the task of identifying the future strategic context for the next thirty years of defence and security, they anticipate that it is highly likely that the governments of rich nations will be continually preoccupied with managing unprecedented events of global humanitarian catastrophe, and at the same time will be left struggling to quell popular protests at home that are aggravated by a heightened competition for essential resources. A highly toxic combination of famine, disease and escalating levels of military conflict in those regions of the globe that experience the most stress on water supplies is likely to lead to mass migrations of poor populations in search of the means to survive. They predict that whilst working to establish and maintain institutional arrangements for addressing the multiple components of such disasters, the governments of advanced industrial nations will also be forced to contend with heightened levels of political extremism at home as hitherto relatively affluent sectors of the middle classes are made more vulnerable to the volatilities of the world economy.

Whilst on a more optimistic footing they acknowledge that it may still be possible over the long term for new technologies and the nurturing of more humane forms of civil society to create conditions on which to launch a more socially progressive and ecologically sustainable world order; for the time being the DCDC warn that current trends suggest that this is a rather improbable scenario. In the short to medium term (i.e. up to the year 2036), they anticipate that the priorities set for national and international politics will be dominated by drives to establish multilateral frameworks for regulating the world economy and initiatives to devise more effective means to monitor and discipline people's outlooks and behaviours so as to contain outbreaks of civil unrest. On this account we have already entered any era where governments are destined to become more heavily involved in managing global capitalism and will be prepared to adopt more authoritarian measures as a means to uphold conventions of civil society in contexts where conditions of austerity set the order of the day (DCDC 2007).

THE FATE OF SOCIOLOGY

What does the future hold for sociology? Indeed, *is* there a future for sociology in the new age of extremes that is already upon us? In recent years, there has been no shortage of publications addressed to the understanding that whatever now passes for 'sociology' is marked by a distinct lack of agreement over the forms of questioning and terms of debate that should be treated as a central concern. Of course, there has never been any consensus when it comes to the ways sociologists identify the overriding principles and purposes of their research, but one of the striking features of the contemporary scene lies in the extent to which commentators regard this as part of an explanation for the absence of sociological voices within the public sphere. On many accounts, sociologists are increasingly inclined to hold back from offering any strong views on how we should live or what we should do so as to secure our futures. The discipline is now marked by a distinct lack of political imagination and appears to retreat from questions relating to fundamental principles of social justice and the grounds for moral solidarity. Whilst providing a home for multiple specialist subfields and serving as a repository for many expressions of personal discontent, Western sociology does not appear to possess either the intellectual orientation or ethical ambition to make a substantive contribution to debates concerning the forms of economy, politics and society with which we might build a better world.

It seems that, yet again, sociology has arrived at a critical juncture in its history where it must undergo a radical reformation of its character and purpose. If not, then it appears to be set on a course where it will become nothing more than an adjunct of middle-class therapy culture or an increasingly outmoded bridge into outlying fields of academic interest. The world will not stand still while we deliberate the conditions of our existence; if we do not make forthright moves to exercise a hand in creating the possible futures before us, then it is very likely that we shall be overtaken by events that rapidly seal our fate. It is time for a new generation of sociologists to declare what they stand for and to make clear what they stand pitted against.

For my part, I hope to contribute to the redevelopment of a sociology that does not shy away from the task of building 'the humane society' and is driven by the goal of eliminating the bounds of social suffering in all its forms (Wilkinson 2005: 157–68). I place a high value on sociological research that reveals the character of society in lived experience and makes clear the conditions under which this is fixed in place or made to change. I celebrate sociological thinking that presents itself as a guide for social practice. I still believe in the potential for sociology to make a positive difference to the ways we live now. I maintain that it can rehabilitate its 'promise' (Mills 1959). I hold that there is still a great deal within the sociological tradition that is relevant and vital for addressing the moral condition of society and the structures of interest that govern our world. I remain committed to the view that sociology not only helps us to understand our place in history, but also has the potential to serve as a guide for understanding how better histories can be made.

In his essay 'Politics as a vocation', Max Weber ventured to outline the ethical attitude that he deemed appropriate and necessary for those who would venture to have any involvement in public affairs. It was originally presented as a lecture at the University of Munich on 28 January 1919. Germany was reeling under the shock of the devastation wrought by World War One and it was becoming clear that the conditions set by the Paris peace negotiations would leave his country economically crippled and politically humiliated for many years to come. Revolutionary uprisings were sweeping across Europe and had recently taken place in Berlin. Two weeks earlier, two of those leading the Berlin revolts, Rosa Luxemburg and Karl Liebknecht, had been arrested, tortured and executed without trial with bullets to the head. Further uprisings and bloodshed seemed inevitable. The horror and tragedy of these times was also reaching towards new level of extremes in the form of the worst flu pandemic in human history that would eventually kill more people than the war (as many as 50 million worldwide) (Tumpey et al. 2005).

'Politics as a vocation' is an exceptional piece of writing from a sociologist with a passionate concern for politics tempered by an overriding commitment to understanding the fate of humanity within the limits set by history and society. It is a key point of reference for those with an interest in Weber's conception of power, his perspective on the history of Western politics and his analysis of the distinctive attributes of political 'personality'. To my mind, the tone of the lecture is also set by a great deal of mourning and a deep sense of loss, but Weber addresses his social suffering as a context for revealing some basic truths about the task of living for the future through the darkest times. Whilst not flinching from making known to his audience that he regards the future as akin to 'a polar night of icy darkness and hardness', he nevertheless concludes by declaring:

> Politics is a strong and slow boring of hard boards. It takes both passion and perspective. Certainly all historical experience confirms the truth – that man would not have attained the possible unless time and again he had reached out for the impossible. But to do that a man must be a leader, and not only a leader but a hero as well, in a very sober sense of the world. And even those who are neither leaders nor heroes must arm themselves with that steadfastness of heart which can brave even the crumbling of all hopes. This is necessary right now, or else men will not be able to attain even that which is possible today. Only he has the calling for politics who is sure he shall not crumble when the world from his point of view is too stupid or too base for what he wants to offer. Only he who in the face of all this can say 'In spite of all!' has the calling for politics.
>
> (Weber 1948a: 128)

In the years to come, I believe that these words will not only be a fount of wisdom for those with a vocation for politics, but also for those who are privileged to pursue a calling for sociology. Increasingly, I am inclined to think that the geopolitical context in which current sociology will discover its fate has no room for those with less than a full commitment to the task of promoting human health and extending the ties of civil society across the globe. It is in relation to its value as a means to establish and maintain institutions for meeting basic human needs, and in terms of its positive contributions to arenas for securing elementary ties of mutual respect, care and understanding that sociology has a future. I suspect that it will be only in so far as the passion for sociology is at the same time driven by a passion for the fate of our common humanity that it will be provided with a space to continue.

BIBLIOGRAPHY

Adam, B., Beck, U. and Van Loon, J. (2000) *The Risk Society and Beyond: Critical Issues for Social Theory*, London: Sage Publications

Adams, J. (1995) *Risk*, London: UCL Press

Alaszewski, A. (2005) 'Risk communication: identifying the importance of social context', *Heath Risk & Society*, 7(2): 101–5

Alaszewski, A. and Horlick-Jones, T. (2003) 'How can doctors communicate information about risk more effectively?', *British Medical Journal*, 327: 728–31

Alcamo, J., Henrichs, T. and Rösch, T. (2000) *World Water in 2025: Gobal Modeling and Scenario Analysis for the World Commission on Water for the 21st Century*, Center for Environmental Systems Research: University of Kassel

Althakami, A. S. and Slovic, P. (1994) 'A psychological study of the inverse relationship between perceived risk and perceived benefit', *Risk Analysis*, 14: 1085–96

Arendt, H. (1968) *Men in Dark Times*, Harmondsworth: Pelican

Armstrong, D. (1995) 'The rise of surveillance medicine', *Sociology of Health & Illness*, 17(3): 393–404

Atkinson, P. and Coffey, A. (1995) 'Realism and its discontents: on the crisis of cultural representation in ethnographic texts', in Adam, B. and Allan, S. (eds) *Theorizing Culture: An Interdisciplinary Critique After Postmodernism*, London: UCL Press

Ayto, J. (1990) *Dictionary of Word Origins*, Indianapolis: Columbia University Press

Ball, D. J. and Golob, L, (1999) 'Diverse conceptions of risk prioritization', *Risk Analysis*, 2(3): 243–61

Bailey, J. (1988) *Pessimism*, London: Routledge

Barry, J. (1999) *Environment and Social Theory*, London: Routledge

Bauman, Z. (1993) *Postmodern Ethics*, Oxford: Blackwell Publishers

Bauman, Z. (2003) *Postmodern Ethics*, Oxford: Blackwell Publishers

Bauman, Z. (2006) *Liquid Fear*, Cambridge: Polity Press

Beck, U. (1992) *Risk Society: Towards a New Modernity*, London: Sage Publications

Beck, U. (1994) 'The reinvention of politics: towards a theory of reflexive modernization', in Beck, U., Giddens, A. and Lash, S. (eds) *Reflexive Modernization: Politics, Tradition and Aesthetics in the Modern Social Order*, Cambridge: Polity Press

Beck, U. (1995a) *Ecological Politics in an Age of Risk*, Cambridge: Polity Press

Beck, U. (1995b) *Ecological Enlightenment: Essays on the Politics of the Risk Society*, New York: Prometheus

Beck, U. (1997) *The Reinvention of Politics*, Cambridge: Polity Press

Beck, U. (1998) *Democracy Without Enemies*, Cambridge: Polity Press

Beck, U. (1999) *World Risk Society*, Cambridge: Polity Press

Beck, U. (2000a) 'The cosmopolitan perspective', *British Journal of Sociology*, 51(1): 79–105

Beck, U. (2000b) *The Brave New World of Work*, Cambridge: Polity Press

Beck, U. (2002) 'The terrorist threat: world risk society revisited', *Theory, Culture and Society*, 19(4): 39–55

Beck, U. (2004) 'Cosmopolitan realism: on the distinction between cosmopolitanism in philosophy and social science', *Global Networks*, 4(2): 131–56

Beck, U. (2005) *Power in the Global Age: A New Global Political Economy*, Cambridge: Polity Press

Beck, U. (2006) *Cosmopolitan Vision*, Cambridge: Polity Press

Beck, U. and Beck-Gernsheim, E. (1995) *The Normal Chaos of Love*, Cambridge: Polity Press

Beck, U. and Beck-Gernsheim, E. (1996) 'Individualzation and precarious freedoms: perspectives and controversies of a subject-orientated sociology', in Heelas, P., Lash, S. and Morris, P. (eds) *Detraditionalization: Critical Reflections on Authority and Identity*, Oxford: Blackwell Publishers

Beck, U. and Beck-Gernsheim, E. (2002) *Individualization*, London: Sage Publications

Beck, U., Giddens, A. and Lash, S. (1994) *Reflexive Modernization: Politics, Tradition and Aesthetics in the Modern Social Order*, Cambridge: Polity Press

Beck, U. and Willms, J. (2004) *Conversations with Ulrich Beck*, Cambridge: Polity Press

Bellaby, P. (1990) 'To risk or not to risk? Uses and limitations of Mary Douglas on risk acceptability for understanding health and safety at work and road accidents', *Sociological Review*, 38(3): 465–83

Bennett, O. (2001) *Cultural Pessimism: Narratives of Decline in the Postmodern World,* Edinburgh: Edinburgh University Press

Bernstein, P. L. (1998) *Against the Gods: The Remarkable Story of Risk,* New York: John Wiley & Sons

Boholm, A. (1996) 'Risk perception and social anthropology: critique of cultural theory', *Ethnos*, 61(1–2): 64–84

Borrell, C., Muntaner, C., Brenach, J. and Artazcoz, L. (2004) 'Social class and self-reported health status among men and women: what is the role of work organisation, household material standards and household labour?', *Social Science and Medicine*, 58: 1869–87

Bourdieu, P. (1993) *Sociology in Question,* London: Sage Publications

Bourdieu, P. (1999) 'Understanding', in Bourdieu, P. et al. *The Weight of the World: Social Suffering in Contemporary Society,* Cambridge: Polity Press

Boyne, R. (2003) *Risk,* Buckingham: Open University Press

Brenot, J., Bonnefous, S. and Marris, C., (1998) 'Testing the cultural theory of risk in France', *Risk Analysis*, 18(6): 729–39

Burawoy, M. (2000) 'Marxism after Communism', *Theory and Society*, 29(2): 151–74

Burawoy, M. (2003) 'For a sociological Marxism: the complemental convergence of Antonio Gramsci and Karl Polanyi', *Politics & Society*, 31(2): 193–261

Burawoy, M. (2005) '2004 American Sociological Association Presidential Address: for public sociology', *British Journal of Sociology*, 56(2): 259–94

Burchell, G., Gordon, C. and Miller, P. (eds) (1991) *The Foucault Effect: Studies in Governmentality,* London: Harvester Wheatsheaf

Castel, B. (1991) 'From dangerousness to risk', in Burchell, G., Gordon, C. and Miller, P. (eds) *The Foucault Effect: Studies in Governmentality,* London: Harvester Wheatsheaf

Cebulla, A. (2007) 'Class or individual? A test of the nature of risk perceptions and the individualisation thesis of risk society theory', *Journal of Risk Research*, 10(2): 129–48

Chandola, T. (2000) 'Social class differences in mortality using the new UK national statistics socio-economic classification', *Social Science and Medicine*, 50: 641–9

Clark, L. and Short, J. F. (1993) 'Social organization and risk: some current controversies', *Annual Review of Sociology*, 19: 375–99

Coburn, D. (2004) 'Beyond the income inequality hypothesis: class, neo-liberalism and health inequalities', *Social Science and Medicine*, 58: 41–56

Coleman, C. L. (1993) 'The influence of the mass media and interpersonal communication on societal and personal risk judgements', *Communication Research*, 20(4): 611–28

Culbertson, H. M. and Stempel, G. H. (1985) 'Media malaise: explaining personal optimism and societal pessimism about health care', *Journal of Communication*, 35: 180–90

Culpitt, I. (1999) *Social Policy and Risk*, London: Sage Publications

Cutter, S. L. (1993) *Living With Risk: The Geography of Technological Hazards*, London: Edward Arnold

Cutter, S. L., Tiefenbacher, J. and Solecki, W. D. (1992) 'Engendered fears: femininity and technological risk perception', *Industrial Crisis Quarterly*, 6: 5–22

Dake, K. (1992) 'Myths of nature: culture and the social construction of risk', *Journal of Social Issues*, 48(4): 21–37

de Roover, F. E. (1945) 'Early examples of marine insurance', *Journal of Economic History*, 5: 172–200

de Souza Jr., A. B. (2000) 'Emergency planning for hazardous industrial areas: a Brazilian case study', *Risk Analysis*, 20(4): 483–93

Dean, M. (1999a) *Governmentality: Power and Rule in Modern Society*, New York: Sage Publications

Dean, M. (1999b) 'Risk, calculable and incalculable', in Lupton, D. (ed.) *Risk and Sociocultural Theory: New Directions and Perspectives*, Cambridge: Cambridge University Press

Deffeyes, K. S. (2005) *Beyond Oil: The View from Hubbert's Peak,* New York: Hill and Wang

Denney, D. (2005) *Risk and Society,* London: Sage Publications

Department of Economic and Social Affairs (DESA) (2007) *World Population Prospects: The 2006 Revision. Highlights,* New York: United Nations

Development, Concepts and Doctrine Centre (DCDC) (2007) *The DCDC Global Strategic Trends Programme 2007–2036*, www.dcdc-strategic-trends.org.uk

Douglas, M. (1978a) *Implicit Meanings: Essays in Anthropology*, London: Routledge & Kegan Paul

Douglas, M. (1978b) *Cultural Bias*, Occasional Papers 35, London: Royal Anthropological Institute of Great Britain and Ireland

Douglas, M. (1986) *Risk Acceptability According to the Social Sciences*, London: Routledge & Kegan Paul

Douglas, M. (1990) 'Risk as a forensic resource', *Daedalus*, 119(4): 1–16

Douglas, M. (1992) *Risk and Blame: Essays in Cultural Theory*, London: Routledge

Douglas, M. (1996) *Thought Styles: Critical Essays in Good Taste*, London: Sage Publications

Douglas, M. and Wildavsky, A. (1982) *Risk and Culture: An Essay in the Selection and Interpretation of Technological and Environmental Dangers*, Berkeley: University of California Press

Draper, A. and Green, J. (2002) 'Food safety and consumers: constructions of choice and risk', *Social Policy and Administration*, 36(6): 610–25

Durkheim, E. (1973) 'Individualism and the intellectuals', in Bellah, R. (ed.) *Emile Durkheim on Morality and Society*, Chicago: University of Chicago Press

Durkheim, E. (2001) *The Elementary Forms of the Religious Life*, Oxford: Oxford University Press

Durkheim, E. and Mauss, M. (1963) *Primitive Classification*, London: Cohen and West

Elliott, A. (2003) *Critical Visions: New Directions in Social Theory*, Lanham, MD: Rowman and Littlefield

Elliot, A. and Lemert, C. (2006) *The New Individualism. The Emotional Costs of Globalisation*, London: Routledge

Elliott, A. M., Smith, B. H., Penny, K. I., Smith, W. C. and Chambers, W. A. (1999) 'The epidemiology of chronic pain in the community', *The Lancet*, 354: 1248–52

Ellis, R. J. (1993) *American Political Cultures*, Oxford: Oxford University Press

Ewald, F. (1986) *L'Etat Providence*, Paris: Grasset et Fasquelle

Ewald, F. (1991) 'Insurance and risk', in Burchell, G., Gordon, C. and Miller, P. (eds) *The Foucault Effect: Studies in Governmentality*, London: Harvester Wheatsheaf

Ewald, F. (1993) 'Two infinities of risk', in Massumi, B. (ed.) *The Politics of Everyday Fear*, Minneapolis: University of Minnesota Press

Ezzati, M., Lopez, A. D., Rodgers, A., Hoorn, S. V., Murray C. J. L. and the Comparative Risk Assessment Collaborating Group (2002) 'Selected major risk factors and global and regional burden of disease', *The Lancet*, 360(2): 1347–59

Finucane, M. L., Alhakami, A. S., Slovic, P. and Johnson, S. M. (2000) 'The affect heuristic in judgements of risks and benefits', *Journal of Behavioural Decision Making*, 13: 1–17.

Fischoff, B., Watson, S. R. and Hope, C. (1984) 'Defining risk', *Policy Sciences*, 17: 123–39

Fischoff, B., Watson, S. R. and Hope, C. (1995) 'Risk perception and risk communication unplugged: twenty years of process', *Risk Analysis*, 15(2): 137–45

Fischoff, B., Lichtenstein, S., Slovic, P., Derby, S. L. and Keeney, R. L. (1981) *Acceptable Risk*, Cambridge: Cambridge University Press

Fischoff, B., Slovic, P., Lichtenstein, S., Read, S. and Combs, B. (1978)

'How safe is safe enough? A psychometric study of attitudes towards technological risks and benefits', *Policy Sciences*, 9: 127–52

Fiske, J. (1989) *Understanding Popular Culture*, London: Unwyn Hyman

Flynn, J., Slovic, P. and Kunreuther, H. (eds) (2001) *Risk, Media and Stigma: Understanding Public Challenges to Modern Science and Technology*, London: Earthscan

Foucault, M. (1982) 'The subject and power', in Dreyfus, H. and Rabinow, P. (eds) *Michel Foucault: Beyond Structuralism and Hermeneutics*, Chicago: Chicago University Press

Foucault, M. (1984) 'Deux essais sur le sujet et le pouvoir', in Dreyfus, H. and Rabinow, P. (eds) *Michel Foucault: Un Parcours Philosophique*, Paris: Gallimard

Foucault, M. (1991) 'Governmentality', in Burchell, C. Gordon and Miller, P. (eds) *The Foucault Effect*, Hemel Hempstead: Harvester Wheatsheaf

Franklin, J. (1998) *The Politics of Risk Society*, Cambridge: Polity Press

Freudenberg, W. and Pastor, S. K. (1992) 'Public responses to technological risks: toward a sociological perspective', *Sociological Quarterly*, 31(3): 389–412

Fromm, E. (1942) *The Fear of Freedom*, London: Routledge

Fromm, E. (1956) *The Sane Society*, London: Routledge & Kegan Paul

Furedi, F. (2006) *Culture of Fear Revisited*, London: Continuum

Furlong, A. and Cartmel, F. (1997) *Young People and Social Change: Individualization and Risk in Late Modernity*, Buckingham: Open University Press

Gabe, B. (2004) *Ulrich Beck: A Critical Introduction to the Risk Society*, London: Pluto Press

Galobardes, B., Lynch, J. W. and Smith, G. D., (2004) 'Childhood socioeconomic circumstances and cause-specific morality in adulthood: systematic review and interpretation', *Epidemiologic Reviews*, 26: 7–21

Gane, N. (2004) *The Futures of Social Theory*, London: Continuum

Gane, N. and Beck, U. (2004) 'Ulrich Beck: the cosmopolitan turn', in Gane, N. (ed.) *The Futures of Social Theory*, London: Continuum

Gaskell, G., Allum, N., Wagner, W., Kronberger, N., Torgersen, H., Mampell, J. and Bardes, J. (2004) 'GM foods and the misperception of risk perception', *Risk Analysis*, 24(1): 185–94

Giddens, A. (1990) *The Consequences of Modernity*, Cambridge: Polity Press

Giddens, A. (1991) *Modernity and Self-Identity: Self and Society in the Late Modern Age*, Cambridge: Polity Press

Giddens, A. (1992) *The Transformation of Intimacy*, Cambridge: Polity Press

Giddens, A. (1994) 'Living in a post-traditional society', in Beck, U., Giddens, A. and Lash, S. (eds) *Reflexive Modernization: Politics, Traditions and Aesthetics in the Modern Social Order*, Cambridge: Polity Press

Giddens, A. (1998) 'Risk society: the context of British politics', in Franklin, J. (ed.) *The Politics of Risk Society*, Cambridge: Polity Press

Gill, R. (1998) 'Dialogues and differences: writing, reflexivity and the crisis of representation', in Henwood, K., Griffin, C. and Phoenix, A. (eds) *Standpoints and Differences: Essays in the Practice of Feminist Psychology*, London: Sage Publications

Goldblatt, D. (1996) *Social Theory and the Environment*, Cambridge: Polity Press

Gouldner, A. (1978) 'The new class project I', *Theory and Society*, 6(2): 343–89

Gouldner, A. (1979) *The Future of Intellectuals and the Rise of the New Class*, New York: Seabury Press

Graham, H. (ed.) (2000) *Understanding Health Inequalities*, Maidenhead: Open University Press

Granger Morgan, M., Florig, H. K., DeKay, M. L. and Fischbeck, P. (2000) 'Categorizing risks for risk ranking', *Risk Analysis*, 20(1): 49–58

Greden, J. F. (2001) 'The burden of recurrent depression: causes, consequences and future prospects', *Journal of Clinical Psychiatry*, 62(22): 5–9

Gureje, O., Von, K., Michael, G., Simon, E. and Gater, R. (1998) 'Persistent pain and well-being: a WHO study in primary care', *JAMA*, 280: 233–8

Gustafson, P. E. (1998) 'Gender differences in risk perception: theoretical and methodological perspectives', *Risk Analysis*, 18(6): 805–11

Hacking, I. (1990) *The Taming of Chance*, Cambridge: Cambridge University Press

Hacking, I. (1991) 'How should we do the history of statistics?', in Burchell, G., Gordon, C. and Miller, P. (eds) *The Foucault Effect: Studies in Governmentality*, London: Harvester Wheatsheaf

Hallowell, N. (1999) 'Doing the right thing: genetic risk and responsibility', *Sociology of Health & Illness*, 21(5): 597–621

Hallowell, N. (2006) 'Varieties of suffering: living with the risk of ovarian cancer', *Health Risk & Society*, 8(1): 9–26

Hallowell, N., Foster, C., Eeles, R., Arden-Jones, A. and Watson M. (2004) 'Accommodating risk: responses to BRCA1/2 genetic testing of women who have had cancer', *Social Science and Medicine*, 59: 553–65

Hämäläinen, P., Takala, J. and Saarela, K. J. (2006) 'Global estimates of occupational accidents', *Safety Science*, 44: 137–56

Harris (Louis) & Associates (1999) *National Pain Survey 1999*, Rochester, NY: Louis Harris & Associates

Healy, S. (2001) 'Risk as social process: the end of "The Age of Appealing to the Facts"?', *Journal of Hazardous Materials*, 86(1–3): 39–53

Heimer, C. A. (1988) 'Social structure, psychology and the estimation of risk', *Annual Review of Sociology*, 12: 491–519

Heinberg , R. (2007) *The Party's Over: Oil, War and the Fate of Industrial Societies*, Forest Row, East Sussex, UK: Clairview Books

Helweg-Larsen, M. and Shepperd, J. A. (2001) 'The optimistic bias: moderators and measurement concerns', *Personality and Social Psychology Review*, 5: 74–95

Henriksen, M. and Heyman, B. (1998) 'Being old and pregnant', in Heyman, B. (ed.) *Risk, Health and Health Care: A Qualitative Approach*, London: Arnold

Heyman, B. (1998) 'Introduction', in Heyman, B. (ed.) *Risk, Health and Health Care*, London: Arnold

Heyman, B. and Henriksen, M. (1998) 'Probability and health risks', in Heyman, B. (ed.) *Risk, Health and Health Care*, London: Arnold

Honneth, A. (2004) 'Organized self-realization: some paradoxes of individualization', *European Journal of Social Theory*, 7(4): 463–78

Hood C., James, B. O., Peters G. and Scott C. (eds) (2004) *Controlling Modern Government: Variety, Commonality and Change*, Cheltenham: Elgar

Horowitz, I. L. (1993) *The Decomposition of Sociology*, New York: Oxford University Press

Hung, H. (2008) 'Rise of China and the global overaccumulation crisis', *Review of International Political Economy*, 15(2): 149–79

Hutton, W. and Giddens, A. (2000) *On the Edge: Living with Global Capitalism*, London: Jonathan Cape

Intergovernmental Panel on Climate Change (IPCC) (2007) *Climate Change 2007: The Fourth Assessment Report*, Geneva: United Nations

Irwin, A. (2001) *Sociology and the Environment*, Cambridge: Polity Press

Irwin, A., Simmons, P. and Walker, G. (1999) 'Faulty environments and risk reasoning: the local understanding of industrial hazards', *Environment and Planning A*, 31: 1311–26

Jackson, R. P. (1990) 'From profit-sailing to wage-sailing: Mediterranean owner-captains and their crews during the commercial revolution', *Journal of Economic History*, 18(winter): 605–28

Jaeger, C. C., Renn, O., Rosa, E. A. and Webler, T. W. (2001) *Risk, Uncertainty and Rational Action*, London: Earsthscan

Jallinoja, P. and Ayro, A. R. (2000) 'Does knowledge make a difference? The association between knowledge about genes and attitude toward gene tests', *Journal of Health Communication*, 5: 29–39

Jones, D. S. (2008) 'Talking and taking risks: an exploration of women's perceptions of antenatal testing in pregnancy', in Petersen, A. and Wilkinson, I. (eds) *Health, Risk and Vulnerability*, London: Routledge

Jones, F. (2008) 'The effects of taxes and benefits on household income, 2006/7', *Economics and Labour Market Review*, 2(7): 37–47

Joslyn, M. R. and Haider-Markel, D. P. (2002) 'Framing effects on personal opinion and perception of public opinion: the cases of physician-assisted suicide and social security', *Social Science Quarterly*, 83(3): 690–706

Kemshall, H. (2002) *Risk, Social Policy and Welfare*, Buckingham: Open University Press

Koestler, A. and Myers, A. (2002) *Understanding Chronic Pain*, Mississippi: University Press of Mississippi

Kreuter, M. W. (1999) 'Dealing with competing and conflicting risks in cancer communication', *Journal of the National Cancer Institute*, 25: 27–35

Kroker, A. and Cook, D. (1988) *The Postmodern Scene: Excremental Culture and Hyper-Aesthetics*, London: Macmillan

Kunst, A. E., Gorenhof, F., Mackenbach, J. P. and the EU Working Group on Socioeconomic Inequalities in Health (1998) 'Morality by occupational class among men 30–64 years in 11 European countries', *Social Science and Medicine*, 46(11): 1459–76

Lasch, C. (1979) *The Culture of Narcissism American Life in an Age of Diminishing Expectations*, New York: Norton

Lash, S. and Urry, J. (1987) *Economies of Signs and Space*, London: Sage Publications

Lash, S. and Urry, J. (1994) *Economies of Signs and Space*, London: Sage Publications

Lash, S., Szerszynski, B. and Wynne, B. (eds) (1996) *Risk Environment and Modernity: Towards a New Ecology*, London: Sage Publications

Leiss, W. (1996) 'Three phases in the evolution of risk communication practice', *The Annals of the American Academy of Political and Social Science*, 545: 85–94

Lemert, C. (1995) *Sociology After the Crisis*, Oxford: Westview

Levine, D. N. (1995) *Visions of the Sociological Tradition*, Chicago: The University of Chicago Press

Leyland, A. H. (2004) 'Increasing inequalities in premature mortality in Great Britain', *Journal of Epidemiological Community Health*, 58: 296–302

Loftedt, R. (2005) *Risk Management in Post-Trust Society*, Basingstoke: Palgrave Macmillan

Loftedt, R. and Frewer, L. (eds) (1998) *Risk and Modern Society*, London: Earthscan

Lubeck, S. and Garrett, P. (1990) 'The social construction of the "at-risk" child', *British Journal of Sociology of Education*, 11(3): 327–40

Luhmann, N. (1991) *Risk: A Sociological Theory*, New York: Walter de Gruyter

Lupton, D. (1999) *Risk*, London: Routledge

Macpherson, C. B. (1962) *The Political Theory of Possessive Individualism: From Hobbes to Locke*, Oxford: Oxford University Press

Marmot, M. (2005) 'Social determinants of health inequalities', *The Lancet*, 365: 1099–104

Marmot, M. and Wilkinson, R. G. (eds) (1999) *Social Determinants of Health*, Oxford: Oxford University Press

Marx, K. (1977 [1851]) 'The eighteenth Brumaire of Louis Bonaparte', in Mclellan, D. (ed.) *Karl Marx: Selected Writings*, Oxford: Oxford University Press

Massumi, B. (1993) 'Everywhere you want to be: introduction to fear', in Massumi, B. (ed.) *The Politics of Everyday Fear*, Minneapolis: University of Minnesota Press

McDaniels, T. L. and Small, M. J. (eds) (2004) *Risk Analysis and Society: An Interdisciplinary Characterization of the Field*, Cambridge: Cambridge University Press

McKenna, F. P. (1993) 'It won't happen to me: unrealistic optimism or illusion of control?', *British Journal of Psychology*, 84: 39–50

Mills, C. W. (1959) *The Sociological Imagination*, Oxford: Oxford University Press

Morgan, K. M., DeKay, M. L., Fischbeck, P. S., Fischoff, B., Morgan, M. G. and Florig, H. K. (2001) 'A deliberative method for ranking risks (II): evaluation of validity and agreement among risk managers', *Risk Analysis*, 21(5): 923–37

Morton, T. A. and Duck, J. M. (2001) 'Communication and health beliefs: mass and interpersonal influences on perceptions of risk to self and others', *Communication Research*, 28(5): 602–26

Mouzelis, N. (1995) *Sociological Theory: What Went Wrong? Diagnosis and Remedies*, London: Routledge

Moynihan, P. J. and Holt, R. D. (1996) 'The national diet and nutrition survey of 1.5–4.5 year old children: summary of the findings of the dental survey', *British Dental Journal*, 181: 328–32

Mutz, D. C. (1992) 'Impersonal influence: effects of representations of public opinion on political attitudes', *Political Behavior*, 14(2): 89–122

Neiman, S. (2002) *Evil in Modern Thought: An Alternative History of Philosophy*, Princeton: Princeton University Press

Noble, T. (2007) 'Family breakdown and social networks', *British Journal of Sociology*, 21(2): 135–50

OECD (2008) *Growing Unequal? Income Distribution and Poverty in OECD Countries*, Paris: OECD Publishing

Office for National Statistics (ONS) (2002) *Psychiatric Morbidity among Adults Living in Private Households, 2000*, London: HMSO

O'Mahony, P. (ed.) (1999) *Nature, Risk and Responsibility*, London: Macmillan Press

O'Malley, P. (1996) 'Risk and responsibility', in Barry, A., Osborne, T. and Rose, N. (eds) *Foucault and Political Reason: Liberalism, Neo-Liberalism and Rationalities of Government*, London: UCL Press

O'Malley, P. (2004) *Risk, Uncertainty and Government*, London: Glasshouse Press

Outhwaite, W. and Ray, L. (2005) *Social Theory and Postcommunism*, Oxford: Blackwell Publishers

Park, E., Scherer, C. W. and Glynn, C. J. (2001) 'Community involvement and risk perception at personal and societal levels', *Health Risk & Society*, 3(3): 281–92

Parsons, T. (1966) 'Introduction', in Weber, M., *The Sociology of Religion*, London: Methuen

Parton, N. (1998) 'Risk, advanced liberalism and child welfare: the need to rediscover uncertainty and ambiguity', *British Journal of Social Work*, 28(1): 5–27

Petersen, A. (1996) 'Risk and the regulated self: the discourse of health promotion as politics of uncertainty', *Journal of Sociology*, 32(1): 44–57

Petersen, A. and Wilkinson, I. (2008) *Health, Risk and Vulnerability*, London: Routledge

Petrou, A., Kupek, E., Hockley C. and Goldacre, M. (2006) 'Social class inequalities in childhood mortality and morbidity in an English population', *Paediatric and Perinatal Epidemiology*, 20: 14–23

Pidgeon, N., Kasperson, R. E. and Slovic, P. (eds) (2003) *The Social Amplification of Risk*, Cambridge: Cambridge University Press

Powell, D. and Leiss, W. (1997) *Mad Cows and Mother's Milk: The Perils of Poor Risk Communication*, Montreal and Kingston: McGill-Queen's University Press

Power, C., Hyppönen, E. and Davey Smith, G. (2005) 'Socioeconomic position in childhood and early adult life and risk of mortality: a prospective study of the mothers of the 1958 British birth cohort', *American Journal of Public Health*, 95(8): 1396–402

Power, M. (2004) *The Risk Management of Everything: Rethinking the Politics of Uncertainty*, London: Demos

Putnam, R. D. (2000) *Bowling Alone: The Collapse and Revival of American Community*, New York: Simon & Schuster

Rayner, S. (1992) ' Culture theory and risk analysis', in Krimsky, S. and Golding, D. (eds) *Social Theories of Risk*, Westport, CT: Praeger

Reading, R. (1997) 'Poverty and the health of children and adolescents', *Archives of Disease in Childhood*, 76: 463–67

Riesman, D. (1950) *The Lonely Crowd: A Study of the Changing American Character*, New Haven, CT: Yale University Press

Rose, N. (1990) *Governing the Soul: The Shaping of the Private Self*, London: Routledge

Rose, N. (1996) 'The death of the social?: refiguring the territory of government', *Economy and Society*, 25(3): 327–64

Rose, N. (1998) *Inventing Ourselves: Psychology, Power and Personhood*, New York: Cambridge University Press

Rose, N. (1999) *Powers of Freedom: Reframing Political Thought*, Cambridge: Cambridge University Press

Royal Society (1992) *Risk: Analysis, Perception and Management*, London: Royal Society

Russell, M., Harris, B. and Gockel, A. (2008) 'Parenting in poverty: perspectives of high-risk parents', *Journal of Children and Poverty*, 14(1): 83–98

Sanders, T. (2004) 'A continuum of risk? The management of health, physical and emotional risks by female sex workers', *Sociology of Health & Illness*, 26(5): 557–74

Savage, M. and Borrows, R. (2007) 'The coming crisis of empirical sociology', *Sociology*, 41(5): 885–99

Savy, P. and Sawyer, A. (2008) 'Risk, suffering and competing narratives in the psychiatric assessment of an Iraqi refugee', *Culture, Medicine and Psychiatry*, 32(1): 84–101

Schilling, C. and Mellor, P. A. (2001) *The Sociological Ambition*, London: Sage Publications

Scholderer, J. and Frewer, L. (2003) 'The biotechnology communication paradox: experimental evidence and the need for a new strategy', *Journal of Consumer Policy*, 26: 125–57

Schwarz, S. and Thompson, M. (1990) *Divided We Stand: Rethinking Politics, Technology and Social Choice*, Hemel Hempstead: Harvester Wheatsheaf

Seidman, S. (1994) *Contested Knowledge: Social Theory in the Postmodern Era*, Oxford: Blackwell Publishers

Sharples, P. M., Sotorey, A., Aynsley-Green, A. and Eyre, J. A. (1990) 'Causes of fatal childhood accidents involving head injury in Northern Region, 1979–86', *British Medical Journal*, 301: 1193–7

Sheeran, P., Abraham, C. and Orbell, S. (1999) 'Psychosocial correlates of heterosexual condom use: a meta-analysis', *Psychological Bulletin*, 125: 90–132

Simmel, G. (1990) *The Philosophy of Money*, London: Routledge

Sjoberg, L. (1997) 'Explaining risk perception: an empirical evaluation of cultural theory', *Risk Decision and Policy*, 2(2): 113–30

Sjoberg, L. (1998) 'Worry and risk perception', *Risk Analysis*, 18(1): 85–93

Sjoberg, L. (2000) 'Factors in risk perception', *Risk Analysis*, 20(1): 1–11

Sjoberg, L., Peterson, M., Fromm, J., Bosholm, A. and Hanson, S. (2005) 'Neglected and overemphasized risks: the opinions of risk professionals', *Journal of Risk Research*, 8(7–8): 599–616

Skeat, Rev. W. (1910) *An Etymological Dictionary of the English Language*, Oxford: Clarendon Press

Skillen, S. L., Olson, J. K. and Gilbert, J. A. (2001) 'Framing personal risk in public health nursing', *Western Journal of Nursing Research*, 23(7): 664–78

Skolbekken, J. (1995) 'The risk epidemic in medical journals', *Social Science and Medicine*, 40: 291–305

Slovic, P. (1987) 'Perception of risk', *Science*, 236(4799): 280–5

Slovic, P. (2000) *The Perception of Risk*, London: Earthscan

Stansfield, S. A. (1999) 'Social support and social cohesion', in Marmot, M. and Wilkinson, R. G. (eds) *Social Deteminants of Health*, Oxford: Oxford University Press

Stenson, K. (1998) 'Beyond histories of the present', *Economy and Society*, 27(4): 333–52

Strydom, P. (2002) *Risk, Environment and Society*, Buckingham: Open University Press

Taylor, S. E. (1989) *Positive Illusions: Creative Self-Deception and the Healthy Mind*, New York: Basic Books

Taylor, S. E. and Armor, D. A. (1996) 'Positive illusions and coping with adversity', *Journal of Personality*, 64(4): 873–98

Taylor, S. E. and Brown, J. (1994) '"Illusion" of mental health does not explain positive illusions', *American Psychologist*, 49(11): 972–3

Taylor, S. E., Kemeny, M. E., Aspinall, L. G., Schneider, S. C., Rodriguez, R. and Herbert, M. (1992) 'Optimism, coping, psychological distress, and high-risk sexual behaviour among men at risk of AIDS', *Journal of Personality and Social Psychology*, 63: 460–73

Taylor-Gooby, P. (ed.) (2000) *Risk Trust and Welfare*, Basingstoke: Macmillan

Taylor-Gooby, P. (ed.) (2004) *New Risks, New Welfare: The Transformation of the European Welfare State*, Oxford: Oxford University Press

Taylor-Gooby and Zinn, J. (eds) (2006) *Risk in Social Science*, Oxford: Oxford University Press

Tenbruck, F. (1989) 'The problem of the thematic unity in the works of Max Weber', in Tribe, K. (ed.) *Reading Weber*, London: Routledge

Therborn, G. (2007) 'Is there a future for the family?', *Public Policy Research*, (March–May): 41–6

Thompson, J. B. (1990) *Ideology and Modern Culture*, Cambridge: Polity Press

Thompson, M., Ellis, R. and Wildavksy, A. (1990) *Cultural Theory*, Boulder, CO: Westview

Tulloch, J. and Lupton, D. (2003) *Risk and Everyday Life*, London: Sage Publications

Tumpey, T. M., Basler, C. F., Aguilar, P. V., Zeng, H., Solórzano, A., Swayne, D. E., Cox, N. J., Katz, J. M., Taubenberger, J .T., Palese, P. and García-Sastre, A. (2005) 'Characterization of the reconstructed 1918 Spanish influenza pandemic virus', *Science*, 310(5745): 77–80

Turner, B. S. and Rojek, C. (2001) *Society and Culture: Principles of Scarcity and Solidarity*, London: Sage Publications

Tversky, A. and Kahneman, D. (1974) 'Judgement under uncertainty: heuristics and biases', *Science*, 185: 1124–31

Tyler, T. T. and Cook, F. L. (1984) 'The mass media and judgements of risk: distinguishing impact on personal and societal level judgements', *Journal of Personality and Social Psychology*, 47(4): 693–708

United Nations (UNDP) (2000/2001), *Human Development Report 2000/2001: Attacking Poverty*, New York: UNDP

United Nations (2003) *Millennium Development Goals: A Compact Among Nations to End Human Poverty*, New York: UNDP

United Nations (2006) *Human Development Report: Beyond Scarcity: Power, Poverty and the Global Water Crisis*, New York: UNDP

United Nations (UN) (2009) *World Economic Situation and Prospects 2009*, New York: United Nations

United Nations Population Fund (UNFPA) (2001) *State of the World Population 2001. Footprints and Milestones: Population and Environmental Change*, New York: UNFPA

Vail, J., Wheelock, J. and Hill, M. (eds)(1999) *Insecure Times: Living with Insecurity in Contemporary Society*, London: Routledge

Veblen, T. (1953) *The Theory of the Leisure Class: An Economic Study of Institutions*, New York: Macmillan

Warner, J. (2008) 'Community care, risk and the shifting locus of danger and vulnerability in mental health', in Petersen, A. and Wilkinson, I. (eds) *Health, Risk and Vulnerability*, London: Routledge

Weber, M. (1948a) 'Politics as a vocation', in Gerth, H. H. and Mills, C. W. (eds) *From Max Weber*, London: Routledge

Weber, M. (1948b) 'The social psychology of the world religions', in Gerth, H. H. and Mills, C. W. (eds) *From Max Weber*, London: Routledge

Weber, M. (1948c) 'Religious rejections of the world and their directions', in Gerth, H. H. and Mills, C. W. (eds) *From Max Weber*, London: Routledge

Weber, M. (1948d) 'Bureaucracy', in Gerth, H. H. and Mills, C. W. (eds) *From Max Weber*, London: Routledge

Weber, M. (1948e) 'Science as a vocation', in Gerth, H. H. and Mills, C. W. (eds) *From Max Weber: Essays in Sociology*, London: Routledge

Weber, M. (1958) *The Protestant Ethic and the Spirit of Capitalism*, New York: Charles Scribner's Sons

Weber, M. (1966) 'Theodicy, salvation and rebirth', *The Sociology of Religion*, London: Methuen

Weber, M. (1978) 'The origins of industrial capitalism in Europe', in Runciman, W. G. (ed) *Max Weber Selections In Translation*, Cambridge: Cambridge University Press

Weinstein, N. D. (1980) 'Unrealistic optimism about future life events', *Journal of Personality and Social Psychology*, 39(2): 186–218

Weinstein, N. D. (1982) 'Unrealistic optimism about susceptibility to health problems', *Journal of Behavioral Medicine*, 5: 441–60

Weinstein, N. D. (1987) 'Unrealistic optimism about susceptibility to health problems: conclusions from a community wide sample', *Journal of Behavioral Medicine*, 10: 481–95

Weinstein, N. D. and Lyon, J. E. (1999) 'Mindset, optimistic bias about personal risk and health-protective behaviour', *British Journal of Health Psychology*, 4: 289–300.

Wheelock, J. (1999) 'Fear or opportunity? Insecurity in employment', in Vail, J. Wheelock, J. and Hill, M. (eds) *Insecure Times: Living with Insecurity in Contemporary Society*, London: Routledge

Wildavsky, A. and Dake, K. (1990) 'Theories of risk perception: who fears what and why?', *Daedalus*, 119(4): 41–59

Williams, R. (1976) *Keywords: A Vocabulary of Culture and Society*, Glasgow: Fontana

Wilkinson, I. (2001a) *Anxiety in a Risk Society*, London: Routledge

Wilkinson, I. (2001b) 'Social theories of risk perception: at once indispensable and insufficient', *Current Sociology*, 49(1): 1–22

Wilkinson, I. (2005) *Suffering: A Sociological Introduction*, Cambridge: Polity Press

Wilkinson, I. (2006) 'The psychology of risk', in Mythen, G. and Walklate, S. (eds) *Beyond the Risk Society: Critical Reflections on Risk and Human Security*, Buckingham: Open University Press

Wilkinson, R. G. (1996) *Unhealthy Societies: The Afflictions of Inequality*, London: Routledge

Wilkinson, R. G. (1999) 'Putting the picture together: prosperity, redistribution, health, and welfare', in Marmot, M. and Wilkinson, R. G. (eds) *Social Determinants of Health*, Oxford: Oxford University Press

Woodroffe, C., Glickman, M., Barker, M. and Power, C. (1993) *Children Teenagers and Health: The Key Data*, Buckingham: Open University Press

World Bank (2000) *Entering the 21st Century: World Development Report 1999/2000*, New York: Oxford University Press

World Bank (2006) *World Development Report 2006: Equity and Development*, New York: Oxford University Press

World Bank (2008) *Rising Food and Fuel Prices: Addressing the Risks to Future Generations*, New York: World Bank

World Health Organisation (WHO) (1999) *The World Health Report 1999: Making A Difference*, Geneva: World Health Organisation

World Health Organisation (2001) *The World Health Report 2001, Mental Health: New Understanding, New Hope*, Geneva: World Health Organisation

World Health Organisation (2002) *The World Health Report 2002 – Reducing Risks, Promoting Healthy Life*, World Health Organisation: Geneva

World Health Organisation (2008) *Closing the Gap in a Generation: Health Equity Through Action on the Social Determinants of Health*, Geneva: World Health Organisation

Wynne, B. (1996) 'May the sheep safely graze? A reflexive view of the expert-lay knowledge divide', in Lash, S., Szerszynski, B. and Wynne, B. (eds) *Risk Environment & Modernity: Towards a New Ecology*, London: Sage Publications

Yeatman, A. (1987) 'The concept of public management and the Australian state in the 1980s', *Australian Journal of Public Administration*, 46(4): 339–56

Zinn, J. and Taylor-Gooby, P. (2006) 'Risk as an interdisciplinary research area', in Taylor-Gooby and Zinn, J. (eds) *Risk in Social Science*, Oxford: Oxford University Press

INDEX